Qualities of God's Servants

Qualities of God's Servants

Lance Lambert

LANCE LAMBERT MINISTRIES

Richmond, Virginia, USA

ISBN: 978-1-68389-036-2

www.lancelambert.org

Contents

Introduction 7

1. Utter Devotion and Implicit Faith 9

2. God's Purpose and Objective 43

3. Abiding 73

4. The Trial of Faith 105

5. Appropriating What is Ours in Christ 121

*Unless otherwise indicated, Scripture quotations
are from the American Standard Version 1901*

Introduction

In the mid 1960's many in the body of Christ were seeking the Lord for reviving. Amongst those praying to the Lord was a group of intercessors in Richmond, England at Halford House. Lance Lambert was amongst this gathering and the Lord was stirring and giving burden to the saints to pray. As time would tell, they were among the many intercessors who prayed, preparing the way for the Jesus movement.

In this same season, Lance shared on qualities God gives to those who He calls to serve Him. You will find within these pages an exhortation to utter devotion to the Lord, the One who supplies all our need. This encouraging word of the fulness of Christ is sure to stir up our faith to rest on what He has done, and to walk in His life rather than our own. And once we have tasted of this life, we will want to remain in it until He comes again!

1.
Utter Devotion and Implicit Faith

We are going to speak about some, and only some, essential characteristics that are to be found in those who would serve God. Of course, there is a sense in which every one of us is called to serve God; that is the most fundamental and basic sense of service. Every single child of God who is born of God's Spirit is called to serve the Lord. We must, therefore, remember that what we say here, in a sense, does apply to every single one of us. However, there are those who are chosen, and appointed, and called to be leaders, perhaps as pioneers in God's work, and in their lives these things must be exemplified. These characteristics must be clearly apparent in the lives of those who in a way are leaders in God's work. Sometimes we call them full-time workers, but really all of us ought to be full-time workers for God. We are all full-time servants of the Lord. It is a great mistake to make a division between full-time servants of the Lord and I suppose part-time servants of the Lord. I do not know what the rest are. There is no such thing in God's Word. We are all full-time servants of the Lord. Some of us are called to serve Him in our homes. Some are called to serve Him in our offices and factories and schools or hospitals. Others are called to serve Him in the work of God, either here in this country or overseas.

Another little point we ought to make before we start is that there is no such thing in God's sight as a mission field and a home field. God has said in His Word: "The field is the world." And we have only to go into London to see that we have the jungle in London in spiritual character, if not in so many leaves, bushes, trees, and animals. The world is the field and it is up to God to appoint where He will have us in the field, where He would have us work for Him. The Lord Jesus said, "Go ye therefore, and preach the gospel to all nations, and make disciples of all the nations, baptizing them into the name of the Father and of the Son and of the Holy Spirit: … and lo, I am with you always, even unto the end of the world" (see Matthew 28:19–20). This is our commission, not the commission of a certain type of God's child called a missionary, but in fact it is the commission to every one of us. However, there have been those who have committed themselves to the Lord in a new way and have told the Lord they are prepared to go anywhere in the world if He should so show them. You, yourself may be getting a little direction as to perhaps where the Lord could be leading you. So we want to talk, very simply, about those characteristics that God looks for in those who would serve Him.

Utter Devotion to Christ

The first characteristic is what I call an utter devotion to Christ, leading to worship, service, and testimony. Matthew 22:34–40: "But the Pharisees, when they heard that he had put the Sadducees to silence, gathered themselves together. And one of them, a lawyer, asked him a question, trying him: Teacher, which is the great commandment in the law? And he said unto him, Thou shalt love the Lord thy God with all thy heart, and with all thy soul, and with all thy mind. This is the great and first commandment. And a second like unto it is this, Thou shalt love thy neighbor as thyself. On these two commandments the whole law hangeth, and the prophets."

The Main Spring of True Worship, Service, and Testimony

This is a most remarkable statement of the Lord Jesus, for He really, virtually said that two-thirds or more of the Old Testament are explained by these two commandments, and they hinge on the keeping of these two commandments. "Thou shalt love the Lord thy God." And secondly, "Thou shalt love thy neighbor as thyself." The main spring of all true worship, service, and testimony, whether here in this country or overseas, is to be the love of God. It is first that love toward the Lord, which becomes absorbed with the Lord, and not only absorbed and captivated by the Lord, but becomes involved with the Lord and identified with the Lord. This is why in that first great letter that Paul wrote to the church at Corinth, where he had so much to say about various disorders, problems, and difficulties, we find this in the 13th chapter: "If I speak with the tongues of men and of angels, but have not love, I am become sounding brass, or a clanging cymbal. And if I have the gift of prophecy, and know all mysteries and all knowledge; and if I have all faith, so as to remove mountains, but have not love, I am nothing" (vv. 1–2).

These are very strong words. Think of it! You could spend twenty years studying theology, you could have all the knowledge about God and all the knowledge about the Bible that is possible to contain, but if you have not love, God's estimate is that there is nothing there. It is futile. Many of us would not go so far as that and say it is futile. For instance, do we know all mysteries? There is not a person in this world that has knowledge of all mysteries, let alone has all knowledge about things that are clearly apparent in God's word.

The cry of our hearts is to have more faith, but God says if we have faith so that we can remove mountains into the sea and yet love is not the main spring, it is futile. It does not mean anything. We do not like this estimate. It is something that we so often seek to avoid. If we had all this great amount of faith, we would be very pleased with ourselves, and I am sure we would say: "Well, I am not very good on love, but I have an awful lot of faith and I can change things and transform things by my faith. But God says, "You can have all faith like that, a practical faith, not a mental faith, but a faith in my heart which can move things and transform things, but if love is not the main spring, it does not mean anything to God. That is a very, very searching and acid test.

Verse 3 goes on: "And if I bestow all my goods to feed the poor, and if I give my body to be burned, but have not love, it profiteth me nothing." There is a progression—preaching, to knowledge of mysteries, to knowledge about God and the things of God, on to faith which can remove mountains.

Then, when God starts to touch our pockets, He is starting to touch our inward being, and He says, "If we bestow all our goods to feed the poor but have not love ..." In other words, if we do it as a good work, as a kind of philanthropist, without real love, it means nothing to God.

The final thing of all is "if I give my body to be burned." In other words, I am going to be a martyr, according to Paul. The last, most final thing we can do is to give our body to be burned, to become a martyr for the faith, but if love is not the main spring behind it, God still says that His estimate of it is futile; it means nothing. When we realise that, we begin to understand something of the nature of love in God's eyes. It is the one thing He looks for.

Of course when Paul wrote this letter, there were no verses and no chapters and it is very interesting to see that Paul was talking about the church in 1 Corinthians 12—that wonderful chapter about the church, which is the body of Christ and all the various functions and gifts and so on that are in the body. We are like that, for we have all been given something of the Holy Spirit by which to serve one another and build one another up. We all belong.

In chapter 14, Paul is talking all about gifts and a good deal more about disorder in the gatherings of God's people. But in between these two matters lies this whole matter of love, just as if the Lord was saying, "Oh, you can talk about the church, you can understand the church, you can seek to build up the church, but the only real thing that matters in the end is the love of God—if we have the love of God in our hearts first for Himself, then for one another, and then for the world. That is the heart of the matter. You see, the church means nothing to God unless it is a place of love, a trysting place. That is why in God's Word the church is called the wife of the Lamb, the bride of God because as far as God is concerned there is no meaning to Christianity and no meaning to the work of God unless it stems from love.

In John 21 this is emphasized even more. After the Lord Jesus had risen from the dead, John 21:15–17 says, "So when they had broken their fast, Jesus saith to Simon Peter, 'Simon, son of John, lovest thou me more than these?' He saith unto him, 'Yea, Lord; thou knowest that I love thee.' He saith unto him, 'Feed my lambs.' He saith to him again a second time, 'Simon, son of John, lovest thou me?' He saith unto him, 'Yea, Lord; thou knowest that I love thee.' He saith unto him, 'Tend my sheep.' He saith unto him the third time, 'Simon, son of John, lovest thou me?' Peter was grieved because he said unto him the third time, Lovest thou me? And he said unto him, 'Lord, thou knowest all things; thou knowest that I love thee.' Jesus saith unto him, 'Feed my sheep.'"

It is a very interesting thing that the first thing the risen Lord Jesus ever really said directly to Peter personally were these words: "Lovest thou me?" Here was the chief of the apostles, the one, in one sense, who was the pioneer of the way, and the first thing the Lord Jesus asked of him, the first challenge the risen Christ ever brought to His once back-slidden child, his once back-slidden disciple now recovered, was a challenge as to whether he loved the Lord. The first command He ever gave to him as a result of that challenge and Peter's response was service: "Feed My Lambs," that is the little ones—feed them. Then He said: "Tend my sheep." Lambs and sheep are to be fed and tended. Now feeding and tending are two different things. To feed creatures is one thing, but to tend them is another, for a lot more care goes into tending than feeding. You have to see they get the right diet I suppose, but sheep normally find their own pasture and all the shepherds have to do is lead them and watch over them. But tending them is really a full time job. He has to watch out for the first signs of disease. He has to watch out for the first signs of sheep getting out of the way. He has to especially guard and keep the little ones and see that the bigger creatures do not push them out of the way, keeping them from getting their share of the food once they have been weaned. All this is service and it is interesting that again the Lord puts His finger upon the question of love. I think we can see that it is the main spring of all true service. The love of God within us enables us to serve one another. Just because we love the Lord, we can serve one another.

In Galatians 5:13–14: "For ye, brethren, were called for freedom; only use not your freedom for an occasion to the flesh, but through love be servants one to another. For the whole law is fulfilled in one word, even in this: Thou shalt love thy neighbor as thyself."

Love for the Lord

For those of you who have responded to the challenge to be a servant of the Lord, the first thing I must ask you is: Where is your love for the Lord? Have you left your first love for the Lord?

This is the first and the most fundamental thing in God's service, and if we have to say it to those who respond to this challenge, what must I say to all of us, myself included? Have we left our first love for the Lord? What is the state of your love? If the Lord Jesus, who knows everything about you, *everything about you*, who knows your true condition, were to stand in this room and say to each one of you, "So and so, so and so, lovest thou Me?" What would you say? What would be the response of your heart? Would it be the same as Peter's? You know, the Lord used one word for love and Peter had to come down to another level when he answered Him. What would you say if the Lord stood here in the midst and said to you: "Lovest thou Me?" Yet our love for the Lord is the key to our love for one another. If you do not love God's children, it is a pretty sure and certain thing that you do not love God. This is a key.

Love for the World

Then there is the love for this world as well. In II Corinthians 5:14a Paul says: "For the love of Christ constraineth us." And this word "constrain" is so interesting. It means the love of Christ presses us, as it were; it squeezes us into serving the world. We have this tremendous energy within us which is driving us in our service to those who are not God's children, to those who are outside the fold of God, and it is God's love.

I must say one more thing before we leave this matter, which in many ways illustrates the point. I have a dear friend, a titled lady who, when she was a young woman of twenty-four, heard God's call to go to the Arab world and she responded. She was a very wealthy woman, a titled woman, and she had recently lost her husband. She responded to God's call but it was very humiliating for her. She did not quite know how a titled lady was to become a missionary. However she faced it and decided to apply to a certain mission. She applied to the mission and of course the board of directors asked her to come and see them. There they were, a long table full of old gentlemen. (It was the beginning of the 20th century.) She stood in front of them and they looked at her, and she felt that every eye was weighing her up and down. They began to ask her questions: When were you converted? Why do you want to go to the field? How were you called? She answered them all until one old gentleman asked her: "Do you love the Egyptians?" Quick as a flash she said, "No, I don't." There was a gasp of horror all around the table, and another old gentleman bent forward and said, "You don't love the Egyptians?" "No," she said, "I detest them. They are the only people I find it hard to love." So then an old gentleman said, "Then, how are you going to work amongst them?" "Oh," said my friend, "God has called me, and I am trusting that in obedience to His call He will give me the love that I do not have." Well, I do not like to say this, but she was a titled lady and a wealthy lady, and I am sure no one else would have gotten past that board, but she did. She was accepted into the mission, and she was sent out to Egypt to begin her work.

But far from the Lord giving her love, she found that she did not have it at all when she got to the smells, and the flies, and the dirt and the heat of Egypt. She found that her love, the little that she had for just a few of the folks, fled from her. Finally, she was asked to help a doctor in some villages right out in the delta, and she went with him. When they were in the clinic, an Egyptian came and said that there was a woman who had collapsed outside the village; they did not know whether she was dead or alive, but she was there. So the doctor told my friend to come with him quickly. They found the woman who had a very advanced case of a certain disease which covered her in open ulcers. She was just a bundle of vermin and rags with huge, awful ulcers. My friend told me that the smell of the woman was so revolting that she could hardly get near her. But the doctor bent over and said: "My friend, there is only one thing we can do and that is to give her an injection, and you will have to hold her. She has probably never had an injection before and she may break the needle if you do not hold her." So my friend had to bend down and hold her, and she said she was nearly ill. All of a sudden something within her said, "Kiss her," and she said, "I can't, I will catch something." Suddenly she let go and she kissed what to her was hardly a human being. At that moment God gave her a love for the Egyptians which never left her in the years she spent in Egypt and later in the rest of her life that she spent in India.

This is a little illustration of a fact. It is God's love that gets us through, not our love. Our love can be very sentimental; it can be very choosy; it can decide what it loves and what it does not love. However, God has a love, which when we respond to Him, He can give to us which can carry us right through. Often it is a simple little act that opens to us an experience of God's love. We have to wash one another's feet, and often it is only when we have taken the step, the humiliating step, as it were, of kissing one another, metaphorically speaking, or washing one another's feet that God floods our heart with a true love. I just give that little illustration. It is not a sentimental thing.

Christ as Everything

What does it mean to be utterly devoted to the Lord? It means, I believe, that we must know Christ as first and Christ as last. Christ is beginning and Christ is end. We must know Christ as all, everything. That is what it means really to love the Lord. It does not just mean that you indulge in lovely little poems about the Lord when the mood so takes you, or you get a little sentimental under the pressure of an emotional type of meeting. It does not mean that at all. Love for the Lord means that you deliberately make Him everything in your life. It does not mean that you can throw everything out and make Him all, but it means that you have to take a stand with the Lord that He is going to be everything.

Let me put it more simply. Christ must be your head; Christ must be your life; Christ must be your goal. I am not going to give you all the references for this, but in Colossians 2:19 you will discover this matter of holding fast the Head. That is the first thing. In Ephesians 4:15 it says "Grow up in all things into him, who is the head." We have to find Christ as our Head. That is a very, very difficult operation to find the Lord as Head, but I do not believe anyone can serve the Lord until they have lost their own head and found Christ as their Head. They really have to discover the Lord as their Head and you have to find the Lord as your life. Again this means that you have to lose your own life to find Christ as your life. Paul put it like this in Philippians 1:21: "For me to live is Christ." And in Colossians 3:4 he says, "Christ, who is our life." That is what it means to be utterly devoted to the Lord—to find Him as our Head, to find Him as our life. Then in Philippians 3:14, find Him as our goal—pressing on toward the goal that we may win Christ—the goal, the objective. That is what it really means.

Let me put it another way. To be utterly devoted to Christ means that you have nothing, you find nothing outside of Him, but you discover everything within Him. Some people have this mentality that if they are going to serve the Lord they have to lose everything, and that life becomes mean and narrow and all denial, and drab, and grey, and much else. It is a really miserable, long-mouthed, grey type of existence.

I do not have to say a lot about that! I have never in my life heard singing like I heard recently of "Count your blessings and name them one by one." Nor have I ever seen such uninhibited joy in the singing of it. It did not worry them what it sounded like; the point was they totally enjoyed it. Those folk had given up everything. They do not know what fresh milk tastes like or what fresh bread is like or the many vegetables we enjoy. A sister said to me after the meal on that Sunday afternoon as she slapped her stomach three times, and I will not forget this for years, "All the things that I have been deprived of were there on that table." That is denial.

Naturally speaking, a life lived like that should be grey, sombre, joyless, and full of sacrifice, the heaviness of the way and the cost of it all. But you see what has happened? When people really do God's will they find it perfect, good, and acceptable. For they so discover the Lord that they are delighted in Him, and they have a joy that makes up for everything else that we would feel joy depends upon. What a lesson that is! Take this to heart: find nothing outside of Christ. If you do you will lose your joy, your peace, and your faith.

The whole point is this: you have got to find your family in Him. You have got to let go your home and find it *in* Christ. You have got to let go of your work and find it *in* Christ. You have to let go of friends and find them in Christ. You have to let go of things and find them in Christ. God does not want to deprive you; He only wants to take away from you what will not make you happy. Oh, if we could only learn this lesson that we can have all things in Him. It does not matter what it is. Paul said in 1 Corinthians 3:21b, 22a, 23: "For all things are yours; whether Paul, or Apollos or Cephas, ... All things are yours; and you are Christ's; and Christ is God's." It is all yours. Oh, if you and I could only learn this lesson!

I remember a brother once put it like this: "You remember Moses had a stick, and this stick was what God used again and again to do tremendous things. You will remember that the first thing the Lord told him to do was: "Throw down the stick, Moses." So Moses threw down the stick and it became a serpent. Then the Lord said, "Pick it up by the tail." That is one thing you never do with a snake. You never pick it up by the tail; you pick it up behind the neck. Picking it up by the tail is the most dangerous thing you can do. And Moses must have said, "Look here, Lord, I have lived here for forty years in the desert; I know a thing or two about the desert. Perhaps You have forgotten. You do not pick up vipers by the tail." But he picked it up by the tail and it became a stick again. What was God teaching? The brother said, "We have to learn that in all things we have to throw them down and see their true nature outside of Christ. Then we have to pick them up again in faith and find them in Christ. And then what happens? We find the authority of God. Those things do not control us, but we are above them. All these things can become idols; they can take the place of the Lord. But we will find that in our utter devotion to the Lord we will have to let go of everything outside of Christ and find it all in Him. You can be sure that if you do not find it in Him, it is not for your good. It is not in your best or highest interest, and in the end you will praise the Lord for it. Utter devotion to Christ is the first and the most important thing, leading to worship, to service, and to testimony.

An Implicit Faith in God

The second thing I would like to say that is an essential characteristic in those who would serve the Lord is an implicit faith in God and His Word. Mark 11:22–24: "And Jesus answering saith unto them, Have faith in God. Verily I say unto you, Whosoever shall say unto this mountain, Be thou taken up and cast into the sea; and shall not doubt in his heart, but shall believe that what he saith cometh to pass; he shall have it." (Mark this: "... but shall believe that what he saith cometh to pass; he shall have it.") "Therefore I say unto you, All things whatsoever ye pray and ask for, believe that ye receive them, and ye shall have them."

Faith is the principle upon which we live, not the principle upon which we are merely saved. It is a tremendous thing to be saved through faith: "Believe on the Lord Jesus Christ and thou shalt be saved." Put your trust in Him, commit yourself to Him lock, stock, and barrel and you will be saved. You will come into an experience of His salvation. But it does not say, the just shall be saved by faith. It says in Romans 1:17b: "... but the just shall live by faith." I have always liked J. N. Darby's translation of this verse where he says, "... the just shall live on the principle of faith." The Christian life is on the principle of faith. Nothing can be more emphatically stated! If God looks for love in us, he also looks for faith and faith is not just a gateway; it is the principle upon which we live.

At any point you and I, who have begun to live in Christ, can die if we step off the principle of faith. In other words, like Lot's wife we can become a monument, salt, just preserved. We become static. You are saved, but you just become static because you have stepped back from living on the principle of faith. The assault on our faith is the wisest of all the devil's stratagems. Why? Because he knows that if he can weaken us in faith he gets a foothold within and once he has that advantage then he can work from there. It can happen that if we begin to retreat from this principle of faith, before we know what has happened, we have become only believers in name; we have become unbelievers in practice. It is so simple. It happens to so many because the evil one knows this. This is why we are told in 1 Timothy 6:12: "Fight the good fight of the, faith, lay hold on the life eternal." This is a contest. It is a fight, and you have to fight this good fight and lay hold on life. It is a positive thing; it is an active thing. Faith does not just go on blooming. It has to be watered and cared for. It is a rather unique type of plant which needs a lot of food and a lot of care if it is going to live. You have to fight this good fight of faith, and you have to lay hold on eternal life. Now that does not just happen at the beginning. We know, of course, that we begin in faith, but it is a life-long trusting of the Lord.

Why does the enemy assault our faith? For the simple fact that he knows that once we step back from faith, we step into uncertainty. We lose our authority; we lose our clarity; we become uncertain people, always dithering. Then we step back into negativism. Once you step back from faith, you immediately become negative. You see everything in its sombre black colours and it is all too much; it becomes a great burden. You do not get any of the joy or peace of the way because there is joy and peace in believing, but once you step back from that you lose it all. There is no more courage; but fear. Fear comes from unbelief. Isn't that true? You only have to look at the waves like Peter and you become fearful and you sink. How many of us become fearful people? We become more fearful than the world itself. They look at us and say, "Here are people called Christians and look at them. They are negative. They are fearful. They are uncertain. They are aimless."

Yes, once you step back from faith you have lost your objective. It is clouded over, and you become aimless again and of course it leaves such emptiness. Once you step back from faith, your life supply, your supply line is cut, and your life becomes empty again. This is why the evil one is watching all the time on this question of faith.

Hebrews 11:6: "And without faith it is impossible to be well-pleasing unto God." Impossible to please God! What strong words! It is impossible to please God without faith.

The second thing even more searching is Romans 14:23b: "… whatsoever is not of faith is sin." I say, that is tremendously searching, isn't it?

The Two Trees in the Bible

There are two trees in the Bible, the tree of life and the tree of the knowledge of good and evil. Faith is the principle of the tree of life. Self is the principle of the tree of the knowledge of good and evil. It is very interesting. All that is not of faith is sin. These are very, very somber words—all that does not have its source in faith, which does not spring out of faith, is sin.

I want to illustrate this from the Old Testament. Abraham had two children, Ishmael and Isaac. One sprang out of faithlessness, and one sprang out of faithfulness. One came out of the sin of unbelief, and one came out of the trial of faith. "Whatsoever is not of faith is sin." Those are searching words. They make us realise how fundamental faith is. "The just shall live on the principle of faith."

The Christian life is a progress in faith. That is what it should be. Romans 1:17a: "For therein is revealed a righteousness of God from faith unto faith." It is a progress, "from faith unto faith," just like "grace unto grace." It is a progress. We are supposed to go on from one triumph in faith to another, and every new triumph in faith brings an increase in our Christian life. It brings us into a new and deeper experience of the Lord. That is what it is supposed to be. That is why we quoted that Scripture in 1 Timothy 6:12: "Fight the good fight of faith." It is a contest all the time. Fight it! Lay hold on life! And every time you triumph, something more is yours. Every time you lose, you can be sure you are on the retreat, and the enemy will get you back. Then you will go back and you will go back and you will go back until you are left with your bare salvation and nothing else. Then you will just feel that you are play acting because you believe everything up in your head and you have nothing within. Your experience is a contradiction to what you believe in your head and what you find in the Book. "Fight the good fight of faith; lay hold on eternal life."

In Ephesians 2:8 you will find that "faith is the gift of God." It was a gift to begin with. How were you saved? How was I saved? We were saved through faith. "For by grace have ye been saved through faith; and that not of yourselves, it is the gift of God." Faith is the gift of God. Sometimes people get the idea that it is much easier to become a Christian if you are credulous. If you are one of those very simple people with very simple minds and very, very credulous, it is an easy thing to become a Christian. Of course the evil one knows about credulous people and he has temptations and hindrances for credulous people as much as he has temptations and hindrances for rational people. Really, when you come down to it, faith is the gift of God. Credulity is not faith. Some people can sort of believe in anything. That is not faith. Some people can get led off into this and led off into that and led off into the other. That is not faith, just because you are credulous. It can be a positive hindrance to growing in the Lord. Faith is the gift of God.

I well know this in my own life. People think I am a credulous person. I do not blame them because I suppose I have got a rather simple mind and I suppose they see it. But what I must say is that I have never yet found faith a natural thing. People will say to me sometimes, "It must be lovely to have faith like you all have in Richmond, and so on, as if it is a natural thing. Some people have even told me that because of some of the things they have heard, they think the English must find it naturally easy to believe. There is nothing farther from the truth. Faith is the gift of God. It does not matter what nationality you are, what background you have, or who you are. Faith is still the gift of God.

In 1951, the largest sum of money we had ever believed for was thirty pounds. When I think of all the sums we have trusted the Lord for and seen come in, and all the things we have seen Him do in answer to faith, I can say this, and God knows and can bear witness to it: I find it as hard now to trust for ten shillings, as it was in 1951.

We are natural unbelievers, and even when God provides, we still immediately wonder: How did it come? Oh, it must have come this way or it must have come that way. Somehow there must be a natural explanation for it. We are natural unbelievers even when we see God work; but God can give us the gift. If we will only exploit and use the grain of faith that is in us by the Holy Spirit, God will give us more and more faith and we can become strong in faith, giving the glory to God. We can come into that wonderful position of seeing ourselves as unbelievers in one sense, and yet knowing the faith of God working in us on the other hand so that there is a paradox of work within. I cannot explain it, but I can tell you that faith is the gift of God. Every single advance, corporate or personal, begins with faith. Do remember that. I do not know where you stand, but let me ask you a question very straightly: Have you been going on from faith unto faith in your life? Has there been an advance or has there been a retreat?

The Witness of A.T. Pierson

I have here one or two witnesses, and I am going to bring them back, as it were, from the dead. They are in the glory. Here is a little part from one of them that has always been a great blessing to me. It is from A. T. Pierson's book *The Bible and Spiritual Life*. It is a wonderful book.

"But let it be observed that this bearing witness to God always implies a risk or *venture*. There is an abandonment of self to God, and *in this mainly the witness consists*. Noah withstood a corrupt and unbelieving world and risked everything on God's being true. Abraham went out not knowing whither he went, and even laid his son of promise on the altar, trusting God to raise him from the dead. Moses renounced Egypt, with all its treasures and pleasures, and undertook to lead a vast host into a wilderness, depending on God's supply for all needs. In Hebrews 11:32–34, we have a brief resume of the triumphs of faith, and the one great feature in all these lines of witnesses is the risk run, the venture of faith upon God—Gideon, with his three hundred and only lamps and pitchers; Daniel, going unarmed into the lions' den, and the three Hebrew children into the fiery furnace; Jonathan and his armour-bearer daring to advance against a whole garrison; Joshua, trusting God and taking Jericho without a blow struck or any dependence on carnal weapons. Every true servant of God accepts some such adventure for God. That is his way of witnessing, and God always honours such witnessing by proving His faithfulness.

"In faith is found also the potent remedy for all the evils of Materialism, Secularism, Rationalism, Ritualism—whatever hinders individual or church development. It keeps the soul in the attitude of waiting on, and receiving from God. It bends the energies of the saved soul upon that higher foundation found in actual likeness to Christ; and hence whatever is unlike Him or hinders assimilation to Him will be detected and detested. No believer can be absorbed in God-likeness and at the same time engrossed in worldliness. He will see that some things divide attention, divert affection, and make spiritual duties and delights distasteful; and he will naturally turn from them. Godly people are always conspicuous for faith—for simple faith. They begin by the simple receiving from Him of salvation; then they advance a stage further, and learn the secret of reckoning on Him for all He promises and then they find it easy to advance to the point of risking everything for Him whom they find can be reckoned on to keep His Word. His truth is his truth." Isn't that beautiful? His truth is his truth.

"From first to last, then, faith is the secret. It makes Salvation ours by approbation; it makes Sanctification ours by simulation; it makes Service ours by co-operation and identification." That is A. T. Pierson. He was a man of faith; he knew what he was talking about.

Faith in God's Word

John 1:1: "In the beginning was the Word." Now this, of course, speaks of Christ as the Word of God, but I am quite sure that there is a connection between Christ as the living Word of God and what we call the Scriptures which are only the manifestation of Him. There is a link between these two. If we have faith in God, we have faith in God's Word. We must see the link between Christ and His Word.

John 14:6: "Jesus saith unto him, I am the truth." In John 17:17 He prayed: "Sanctify them in the truth; thy word is truth." Jesus is the truth. "... the truth as it is in Jesus," says Paul. And He speaks of them: "Sanctify them in the truth; thy word is truth." There is a link between the risen Christ and the written Word.

Look at I Peter 1:11: "Search what time or what manner of time the Spirit of Christ which was in them did point unto, when it testified beforehand the sufferings of Christ, and the glories that should follow them." Why doesn't God's Word say the Spirit of God? Why does it say that it was the Spirit of Christ who was the divine author of the Bible? He was in the prophets speaking, as it were within them, these words that have come to be called the Bible.

Again in II Peter 1:16a:

"For we did not follow cunningly devised fables,
when we made known unto you the power
and coming of our Lord Jesus Christ."

"And we have the word of prophecy made more sure;
whereunto ye do well that ye take heed, as unto a lamp
shining in a dark place, until the day dawn, and the
day-star arise in your hearts: knowing this first, that no
prophecy of scripture is of private interpretation. For no
prophecy ever came by the will of man: but men spake from
God, being moved by the Holy Spirit" (verse 19–21).

Faith in God means faith in God's Word. We take what God has said, we appropriate it, we believe it, and we see it realised. St. Augustine put it like this: "Become what you are." Now that may take some explaining, but really he simply was saying, "You are sanctified, become sanctified. You are crucified; become crucified. You are seated in the throne, then come to that. Become what you are."

We have once or twice read a little portion in Erich Sauer's book, *From Eternity to Eternity*. I thought I would read it again because in many ways it is a rather wonderful little note on inspiration and I think it is rather remarkable. "We believe in a full inspiration as worthy of God in the view of the fact that in the Creation, which is the Divine revelation in Nature, the minutest objects are ordered with the greatest care and exactness.

"From its greatest representatives in the starry world down to the minutest creatures and plants, indeed to the molecules, atoms and electrons of which it is composed, Nature is built up with inconceivable exactness according to most refined and powerful laws. Therefore we ask, Shall the Most High, seeing that He is so wonderfully ordered in the lower form of His self-revelation, that is, in Nature, have employed less care in the infinitely higher and nobler revelation, that is, His testimony in the written Word?

Every butterfly wing with its hundred thousand pellicles; the eye of every fly with its six to seven thousand lenses; every spider thread, with its 300 single threads, is a witness to this exactness and the 306 armour plates of a beetle, the 8,000 pairs of muscles of a silkworm, the 700 strokes per second of the wings of a gnat, the sperms of the 300,000 species of mushroom which are so minute that one of each sort would not even fill one thimble—are they not all a direct, irrefutable proof that not only is it not unworthy of God, the Greatest of all, to control the tiniest of all things, but that, on the contrary, it most fully and in the highest degree, displays His greatness? Or we may think of the marvellous structure of the bee, 31,000 sensitive hairs are on the feelers of the drone, 5,000 facets (of lenses) are set together in each eye of the bee, all exactly hexagonal. The 440 strokes of the wing per second enable it to attain a speed of forty miles per hour, almost the average speed of a fast train and finally, what shall we say of the Infusoria, some of which are so small that of one variety in Bohemia, not less than 225 million armour plates are found in one single cubic centimeter? To say nothing of the marvellous power of that ten thousandth gramme of animated matter which we call the brain of the ant, or of the wholly inconceivable atomic planetary systems which are the basis of matter, or of the other millions upon millions of wonders of the tiny world of the most minute things. Lastly, seeing that, as the Lord said, the very hairs of our head are all numbered, (Mt. 10:30) will God be less concerned as to the details of His Word by which He wishes to guide millions of human beings with unending existence, to salvation, blessedness, and glory in all the ages of eternity?"

Whatever you may think about that, it has some truth in it. If God has shown such care over small things, then we can trust this Book. There are some things that we cannot explain. There are some things as yet we cannot fully reconcile, but oh, the wonder of this Book when it is taken in its over-all pattern—its theme, its harmony, its cohesion, its unity. It is remarkable! I have never yet discovered a person who has a question about this Book who is being really used by God. That is a very, very strong thing to say. I have met many people with questions about this Book. I have met them on the mission field, I have met them at home, and I have always found them dear people, cultured people often, but people who have lost their certainty, lost their clarity, and lost very much of their experience. No, this Book is entirely trustworthy and the greatest evidence for its trustworthiness is the fact that those who trust God's Word find it works. You can trust every one of its promises.

Quotes from C. T. Studd

Last night in a time of prayer a brother read to us a little portion from C. T. Studd. Of course, C. T. Studd was the father of all those who came this last weekend, and this is the book through which God saved me. As a result of his reading it, I took it up today. Once again, after all these twenty years, I was immersed in this book, which when I was a lad of twelve led me to Christ. I want to read to you just three things from a man who gave up a fortune, was one of the co-team members with W. G. Grace, one of the great English cricketers, and went up to China and to India. When he should have retired, he finally went to Africa. Mary Rees and I have laughed together at the thought of dear old C. T., in the glory, as now he sees literally thousands upon thousands of souls who have come to Christ through his faith. These are some of the things he said when, it is hard to believe it, Central Africa was all cannibal territory and when there was hardly any missionary work there at all.

"Too long," he said in a letter just before he went out to Africa, "we have been waiting for one another to begin. The time for waiting has past. The hour of God has struck. War is declared! In God's holy name let us arise and build. The God of heaven will fight for us as we for Him. We will not build on the sand but on the bedrock of the sayings of Christ, and the gates and minions of hell shall not prevail against us. Should such men as we fear?

"Before the whole world, aye, before the sleepy, lukewarm, faithless, namby-pamby Christian world, we will dare to trust our God. We will venture our all for Him. We will live and we will die for Him, and we will do it with His joy unspeakable singing aloud in our hearts. We will a thousand times sooner die trusting only in our God than live trusting in man, and when we come to this position, the battle is already won and the end of the glorious campaign in sight. We will have the real holiness of God, not the sickly stuff of talk and dainty words and pretty thoughts. We will have a masculine holiness; one of daring faith and works for Jesus Christ."

Here is another letter. This was written to his great friend Dr. Wilkinson just before he went out to Africa. This is just when he was going to start the Heart of Africa Mission.

"The committee I work under is a conveniently small committee, a very wealthy committee, a wonderfully generous committee, and is always sitting in session—the committee of the Father, the Son and the Holy Ghost.

"We have a multimillionaire to back us up, out and away the wealthiest Person in the world. I had an interview with Him yesterday. He gave me a cheque-book free and urged me to draw upon Him. He assured me His Firm clothes the grass of the field, preserves the sparrows, counts the hairs of the children's heads. He said the Head of the Firm promised to supply all our need and to make sure, One of the Partners or rather Two were to go along with each member of our parties, and would never leave us or fail us. He even showed me some testimonials from former clients. A tough old chap with a long beard and hard bitten face said that on one occasion supplies had arrived and been delivered by black ravens, and on another, by a white winged angel. (He was referring to Elijah of course.) *Another little old man who seemed scarred and marked all over like a walnut shell,"* (This is the apostle Paul.) *"said he had been saved from death times untold for he had determined to put to proof the assurance that he who would lose his life for the Firm's sake should find it. He told stories more wonderful than novels and Arabian nights, of escapes and hardships, travels and dungeons, and with such a fire in his eye and laugh in his voice, added, 'But out of all of them the Partner delivered me.' He said gambling for Christ was the best game in the world. He said the compulsory rest cure now was rather hard on him with his gambling craze still there, but the Chief Partner commanded it, and said he must not be selfish and greedy about it, that he had good long innings and made the highest score so far, and had better sit quiet a bit, with pads off and coat on, and encourage the others. It did me good to see this old warrior. He was like a bit of red-hot*

quicksilver and one felt scorched up with shame—and ever
since I saw him, and heard him, I have had a sort of pocket
telephone inside, ringing me up and saying at intervals, 'Go
it, old chap; go in for a slog. Your eye's in all right, and their
bowling is getting weak. Take the long handle, only a few
minutes till the stumps are drawn. Go to it! Bravo! Now go!"

Now you can understand why C.T. Studd was disliked by so
many Christians. He was a man who did not mince words, and
although he was an aristocrat he upset an awful lot of people.
This is the other portion I am going to read. It shows you the stuff
that men of God are made of who turned the world upside down.
There are some very pretty little saints sometimes, seemingly so,
but here is the stuff that turned the world upside down and really
changes nations.

"When in hand-to-hand conflict with the world and the devil,
neat little biblical confectionary is like shooting lions with
a pea-shooter. One needs a man who will let himself go and
deliver blows right and left as hard as he can hit, trusting in
the Holy Ghost. It's experience, not preaching, that hurts the
devil and confounds the world because it is unanswerable;
the training is not that of the schools, but of the market; it's
the hot, free heart and not the balanced head that knocks the
devil out. Nothing but forked-lightning Christians will count.
A lost reputation is the best degree for Christ's service.

"I am more than ever determined that no ring nor limit
shall be placed around us, other than that of our Lord

Himself, to the uttermost parts, to every creature I
belong and will ever belong to the great God-party. I
will have naught to do with the little God-party.

"*The difficulty is to believe that He can deign to use*
such scallywags as us, but of course he wants faith and
fools rather than talents and culture. All God wants is a
heart, any old turnip will do for a head; so long as we are
empty, all is well, for then He fills with the Holy Ghost.

"*The fiery baptism of the Holy Ghost will change soft, sleek*
Christians into hot, lively heroes for Christ, who will advance
and fight and die, but not mark time. Let us race to heaven;
an accident means dashing into the arms of Jesus—such
accidents are God's choicest blessings. Don't be a luggage train.

"*Fools would 'cut the devil,' (that is cut him out)*
pretending they do not see him; others erect a tablet
over his supposed grave. Be wise; don't cut nor bury
him. Kill him with the bayonet of evangelism.

"*Hugh Latimer was an inextinguishable candle. The devil lit*
him, and ever since has been kicking himself for his folly. Won't
someone else tempt the devil to make a fool of himself again?

"*Nail the colours to the mast! That is the right thing to do,*
and, therefore, that is what we must do, and do it now.
What colours? The colours of Christ, the work He has
given us to do—the evangelization of all the unevangelised.

Christ wants not nibblers of the possible, but grabbers of the impossible, by faith in the omnipotence, fidelity, and wisdom of the Almighty Saviour Who gave the command. Is there a wall in our path? By our God we will leap over it! Are there lions and scorpions in our way? We will trample them under our feet! Does a mountain bar our progress? Saying, 'Be thou removed and cast into the sea, we will march on. Soldiers of Jesus! Never surrender!'

"'But what if C. T. dies?' We will shout 'Hallelujah!' The world will have lost its biggest fool, and with one fool less to handicap Him, God will do greater wonders still. There shall be no funeral, no wreaths, crape nor tears, not even the dead march. Congratulations all round will take place. For he says, 'And I, if I be offered up, rejoice and congratulate you; do ye also rejoice and congratulate me?'(Philippians 2:17–18). Our God will still be alive and nothing else matters. The first Heart of Africa Mission funeral will take place when God dies, but as that will not be till after eternity, cheer up all. Forward! Every man straight before him. Hallelujah! To die is gain."

This is the famous verse that is often quoted of C. T. Studd: "Some wish to live within the sound of church or chapel bell; I want to run a Rescue Shop within a yard of hell." That is exactly what he did. He went out to the cannibals; he lived there and never came home. He died in very great pain in the end, but triumphantly. And now, all over Central Africa and all over the world, I suppose it must now number some million who have found Christ and whose lives have been transformed by this one old man's faith.

That is the kind of faith you and I have got to have. We may not be the personality that C. T. Studd was, but we have got to have the same faith. We have got to have that faith which can dare and can adventure for God.

Three Things About Faith

There are three things about faith. The first one is: " ... looking unto Jesus, the Author and Finisher of our faith (Hebrews 12:2). How do you get this gift of faith? By looking unto Jesus. Vision always results in faith. If your eye is on yourself, or people, or things, you will not have faith. You have got to look unto Jesus who is the Captain or the Pioneer or the Author of faith, and the Perfecter. That is the One who develops it, finishes it, and perfects it—the Perfecter of our faith. If you go on to serve God, you must learn to look unto Jesus. This is the most important thing of all. If you look at people, if you look at things, if you look at co-workers, if you look at the work, you will go down. You have got to learn to look unto Jesus. Everything else breeds unbelief. Everything else. Even our dearest and most cooperative brothers and sisters can breed unbelief in us if we get our eyes on them. We have got to look off to Jesus.

The second thing, if you want to know an implicit faith in God and His Word, is Romans 10:17: "Faith cometh by hearing and hearing by the Word of God." Let me put it very simply: Faith cometh by the Word of God. How does faith come? It comes when you study this Book with the help of the Holy Spirit.

When you have a reverent and humble approach to this Book, faith comes. I do not believe faith comes first that way; it comes by hearing. But it is true that our faith is fed by feeding on God's Word, believing and trusting God's Word.

Finally, faith is the gift of God as we have said, and in Galatians 2:20 there is a very interesting phrase. In the AV, which I think is better than the RSV, it says, "I live by the faith of the Son of God." That is a very lovely phrase. Sometimes we do not have any faith, but then we can trust the Lord.

Hudson Taylor's Experience

Hudson Taylor, the founder of the China Inland Mission, went through three experiences in his life, so he tells us in that little tiny book called *A Retrospect*. The first was that he had no faith when he was young. He only had faith to trust the Lord for his salvation, but he had no faith for anything else nor did he think it was required. He used to have a salary and everything else when he first went out to the field, to China, which had been a closed country that had just opened.

Then, he went to his second experience where he saw that all could be opened by faith. God had provided everything; faith was the key. If you only had the faith, you could experience as much as your faith would allow you to.

As he got older in the Lord, he had some very dark experiences and he lost his faith. He had not lost his faith in the Lord, but he lost his faith to trust the Lord for his every-day provision. He went through a very terrible time. (If any of you have read the book, *Hudson and Maria*, [his first wife] a beautiful account, you will have read it there). He went through a very deep and dark patch and one day he just felt that everything had come to an end, and he did not seem to be able to screw up enough faith to trust the Lord. He thought of his children, he thought of his wife, and he thought it must be the end.

He did not give up reading God's Word; in his depression he read it. In II Timothy 2:12, he came across this: "If we suffer with him, we shall also reign with Him: if we deny him, he will deny us: if we are faithless, he abideth faithful." He suddenly realised that it was the faith of the Son of God that was going to get him through—not his own faith even. His own faith was necessary; it was vital, but in the end it was God's faith, the faith of the Son of God that was going to get him through. From that day on he found that the Lord was always there. Even when he found himself weak in faith, he found that underneath were the everlasting arms.

You must have an implicit faith in God and in His Word. There are only two things to remember: an utter devotion to the Lord leading to worship, service, and testimony, and an implicit faith in God and in His Word. These two are essential characteristics that God looks for in all who would serve Him.

2.
God's Purpose and Objective

The second of these special studies is really a little bit of advice to those who would serve God. The last time we spoke about two things only. The first was that God looks for certain characteristics in those who would serve Him. Of course, in a sense, we are all serving the Lord, but there are those who are called to go forth and serve Him in His work. We all serve Him in the office, our home, wherever God has placed us, but some are called to serve Him in an especial way, and God looks for certain characteristics in them. The first one we dealt with was an utter devotion to Christ leading to worship, service, and testimony. The second thing we spoke about was an implicit faith in God and in His Word.

The third characteristic that God looks for is a clear understanding of God's purpose and objective. God has an eternal purpose. He has an objective of the ages. All down through the ages before even time began, God had a purpose and an objective. When time started and the Fall came, it has not altered that purpose and objective of God. And this is very, very important for us to understand. Let's look at a number of Scriptures.

The Mystery Hidden in God

"Who saved us, and called us with a holy calling, not according to our works, but according to his own purpose and grace, which was given us in Christ Jesus before times eternal." Let's underline this phrase: *according to His own purpose which was given us in Christ Jesus before times eternal.* II Timothy 1:9

"And we know that to them that love God all things work together for good, even to them that are called according to his purpose." We are called according to His purpose. Romans 8:28

"For he (God) has made known to us in all wisdom and insight the mystery of His will according to His purpose which he set forth in Christ as a plan for the fullness of time to unite all things in Him, things in heaven and things on earth. In Him according to the purpose of Him who accomplishes all things according to the counsel of His will, we who first hoped in Christ as being destined and appointed to live for the praise of His glory." Ephesians 1:9–12 (ARSV)

Here you have a fuller explanation of this phrase "His purpose." We are told it is the mystery of God's will according to His purpose which He set forth in Christ. And what is it? "As a plan for the fullness of time to unite or head up or sum up all things in Him, things in heaven and things on earth." Then we discover that we are in Him. Verse 12: "We who first hoped in Christ have been destined and appointed to live for the praise of His glory."

> *"And to make all men see what is the plan of the mystery hidden for ages in God who created all things, that through the church the manifold wisdom of God might now be made known to principalities and powers in the heavenly places. This was according to the eternal purpose which he had realised in Christ Jesus our Lord." According to the eternal purpose which He has realised in Christ Jesus our Lord. Note again, the plan of the mystery hidden for ages in God. Ephesians 3:9–11 (ARSV)*

> *"Now unto him that is able to establish you according to my gospel and the preaching of Jesus Christ, according to the revelation of the mystery which have been kept in silence through times eternal." Romans 16:25*

I want you to underline especially the word mystery, the revelation of the mystery which has been kept in silence through times eternal.

We have already read in Ephesians 3:9: "... to make all men see what is the plan of the mystery hidden for ages in God." We have this phrase again in Romans 16:25: "According to the revelation of the mystery which has been kept in silence."

In Ephesians 3:3–6 these Scriptures are interpretations of one another. Paul said, "How that by revelation was made known unto me the mystery, as I wrote before in few words, whereby, when ye read, ye can perceive my understanding in the mystery of Christ;

which in other generations was not made known unto the sons of men, as it hath now been revealed unto his holy apostles and prophets in the Spirit; to wit, that the Gentiles are fellow-heirs, and fellow-members of the body, and fellow-partakers of the promise in Christ Jesus through the gospel."

Now just by Scripture alone you are coming perhaps to an understanding of this phrase "eternal purpose." It is the same as the mystery. What is it? That we might be fellow-heirs, fellow-members of the body, and fellow-partakers of the promise. That is tremendous.

Colossians 1:26: "Even the mystery which hath been hid for ages and generations: but now hath it been manifested to his saints." (It was to the holy apostles and prophets, now it is to all, to all His saints.) "To whom God was pleased to make known what is the riches of the glory of this mystery among the Gentiles, which is Christ in you, the hope of glory." *Christ in you all, the hope of glory.*

This word mystery is most interesting because it does not mean what we mean by mystery. When we talk of something being a mystery, we mean it is hidden; it is veiled. You just cannot understand it because it is a mystery. I might say, "Honestly, he is a mystery to me." And I mean by that he is impenetrable. You just cannot get to know him. He is a mystery or she is a mystery. Or we may say that place is a mystery. What do we mean by that? It is completely veiled, and it is really impossible to discover what is in it. It is a mystery.

However, the scriptural use of this word mystery is quite different and it means literally: "what is known only to the initiated." It is something which is a secret from all others, but is revealed to certain people. In other words, the initiated understand, but to the uninitiated it is nonsense. It is veiled; it just does not make sense. When you begin to understand that, you get to the root of this whole problem of the purpose of God.

Why is it that so few people understand what God's purpose is? I would like to read just a little portion from Vine's New Testament Dictionary of Words because I believe it will help you. Listen very carefully. "In the New Testament this word mystery denotes not the mysterious as with the English word, but that which being outside the range of unassisted natural apprehension can be made known only by divine revelation and is made known in a manner and at a time appointed by God and to those only who are illumined by His Spirit. In the ordinary sense, a mystery implies knowledge withheld. Its scriptural significance is truth revealed."

Fellow-heirs, Fellow Members, Fellow Partakers

God has an eternal purpose. It is realised in Christ Jesus. It is called the mystery hidden for ages and generations. And what is it? That we are fellow-heirs, or fellows in the inheritance, fellow-members of the body of Christ, and fellow partakers in the promise which is in Christ. It is Christ in us.

I Peter 5:10 is a very interesting word indeed. "The God of all grace, who called you unto his eternal glory in Christ." *The God of all grace, who called you unto his eternal glory in Christ.* Then Ephesians 1:12 says, "To the end that we should be unto the praise of his glory."

Peter says we have been called unto His eternal glory in Christ. Paul says, "To the end that we might be a praise unto His glory."

See Revelation 21:10b which says, "And showed me the holy city Jerusalem, coming down out of heaven from God, having the glory of God." Verse 9b: "I will show thee the bride, the wife of the Lamb." The holy city Jerusalem, having the glory of God.

Now, connect all these phrases: The God of all grace has called us unto his eternal glory in Christ. What is the point, the objective of God's purpose? "To the end that we might be unto the praise of His glory." What does this mean? Does it just mean that we should all sort of have a bit of glory to revel in? No. The last time this word glory is used in this connection is in Revelation 21 and 22, and it is clear that it is all connected with the city of God, the bride of Christ, the wife of the Lamb having the glory of God. She is the vessel of God's glory. God's glory has filled her.

"When Christ shall come to be glorified in his saints, and to be marvelled at in all them that believed." II Thessalonians 1:10

That is going to be a wonderful day when Christ comes to be glorified in all His saints." Isn't that wonderful!—glorified in His saints and marvelled at in all them that believed?" Now if you put these Scriptures together you will come to a conclusion. If you study these Scriptures and look through them in your quiet time, I believe God will show you something that is absolutely vital, and it is all in connection with God's eternal purpose. It is vitally important that we should know clearly what that supreme purpose of God is.

The Need to Know God's Eternal Purpose

Now, if I were to ask you: Do you know what God's eternal purpose is? How would you answer? If I were to say to you: Take a small piece of paper and write down in a sentence or two what God's eternal purpose and objective is, could you do it? Could you really do it? I would be most interested to know. I must say that the ignorance there is over the eternal purpose of God appalls me. People say they know what it is. "Oh," they say, "the eternal purpose is wonderful, wonderful!" However, when it comes to putting it in black and white, they cannot do it. Some of them have got to almost write a book, which when they have written it is almost unintelligible.

What really is the eternal purpose of God? You ought to be able to give a reason for the hope that is within you. You ought to be able to put down in a few brief words exactly what God's eternal purpose is and what His objective is. And if you are amongst those whom God is putting His hand on and you are going to go out into His service and work, I cannot stress enough how utterly and vitally important it is that you should know. This knowing does not mean that you can waffle on for hours about it, but that you can put in a few concise words exactly what is the heart of this matter.

If we are not absolutely clear, there is a very real possibility of not only being lost in detail and in much activity, but of being sidetracked altogether. If a man does not know what the objective is in his work, he can easily get sidetracked, can't he? Suppose I give a man a whole lot of bricks and ask him to come here and build something. I also tell him that I have a plan and a purpose.

However, he never asks about it and he just begins building something out in the garden. It is quite clear that he is easily going to get lost in an awful lot of activity. He might build a beautiful great wall with the bricks, which I do not want. He might spend all his energy making a very beautiful little fireplace in one corner, which I have no need for at all, because it is supposed to be a chicken house. That is the purpose of it; I do not even want a fireplace. If you have a purpose and objective, the man has got to know what the material is for. He has got to conserve his energy, so that his energy is channeled into exactly what is going to produce the best result. If he does not know what the design is, if he does not know what the purpose is, if he does not know what the objective is, then there is every possibility he is going make a lot of unnecessary mistakes, a lot of energy is going to be misspent, and a lot of valuable material, as well, is going to be put in the wrong place.

That is a perfect description of Christendom today. There is a tremendous amount of misspent energy. Valuable material mis-appointed, misplaced. Why? Because there is this terrible ignorance as to the purpose of God and to His objective. Of course, you can get sidetracked altogether, and a man might build me a summerhouse when I want a chicken run. He has gotten sidetracked altogether. There may be many features about a summerhouse which he has done very beautifully, but which are of no earthly use to my chickens at all. In fact, it could be positively harmful. So you see, it is all very important to be absolutely clear what God's purpose is.

In every other aspect of life, every single sphere in life, men and women are expected to know what they are about. They are expected to be able to say quite clearly, generally speaking, if they have positions of responsibility, exactly what their purpose of being there is. What is the objective of their work? You do not think much of having a manager, in a firm or factory who cannot put into a few words exactly what the objective of the factory is. It is an amazing thing and I cannot understand why you are expected to know what the objective and purpose is in every sphere of life except in the Christian world. There, evidently, you can do anything. You are rarely asked: "What is this?"

The best answers I have gotten to date, the most general sort of answers I ever had to this question have been like this: "Well, we are saved to serve." That is true, but it is far too broad in one sense. Often when you inquire into exactly what that means, it means very little. Again, you have another question of someone who feels they have scored and they say, "Oh well, it is not only that you are saved to serve, that is important, but beyond that it is the glory of God." But if you asked them what the glory of God is, what does the glory of God mean, they cannot tell you, for it is in many ways a trite phrase, just simply lifted out of Scripture. Now, this is all very important. I am putting it forcefully because I believe it needs to be put very, very forcefully indeed.

For instance, take a big building site in London. Say there are five hundred men working on that building site. Of course, not all those five hundred workers on the building site will know precisely and in detail the plan and design of the building. It stands a very good chance that quite a number of them do not know exactly what is happening. They are told to mix cement, and they mix cement. They are told to bring it from one place and put it in another place, and they do that. However, every single person on that building site with real responsibility knows the plan and is working according to the plan and is responsible to see that everyone else under them is working according to plan even if they do not know it. The man who is told to mix up the cement and bring it here might not know quite honestly what it is for, except it is something to do with the foundation or possibly to do with the brickwork. He does not know much more. It depends possibly on his intelligence and the interest he has. But the person who is directing him and supervising him does know.

This is very important when it comes to God's work, for in a sense, service is like scaffolding around the house of God. It is all the workers and the scaffolding and the instruments being used to build the house, and everyone who is responsible has got to be a builder. And those builders, especially the master builder, all have to know what the plan is. (You will remember that Paul called himself a master builder.) What is the design? Then everything can be coordinated and it all flows together because they have an understanding.

The Battle Over God's Eternal Purpose

Then again, I wonder if we sufficiently realise that we have all been placed on a war footing. I know of course there is a side to the Christian life, and it should be so—a triumphant, joyful, and restful side, but let us make no mistake about it. The whole church has been placed on a war footing at Pentecost. It has been on a war footing ever since. That really is an explanation for the battle that rages backwards and forwards over the true church. It is on a war footing as far as heaven is concerned.

Look again at Ephesians. In this letter of Ephesians we have a tremendous exposition of God's eternal purpose, and how does Paul end this letter? Ephesians 6:10–12: "Finally, be strong in the Lord, and in the strength of his might. Put on the whole armor of God, that ye may be able to stand against the wiles of the devil. For our wrestling is not against flesh and blood, but against the principalities, against the powers, against the world-rulers of this darkness, against the spiritual hosts of wickedness in the heavenly places."

Now that is war. Here you have the whole varied ranks of a satanic army that are gearing up to war, and when we least expect it they can trip us up. If the evil one can lull us into thinking that we are in peacetime when in fact we are in wartime, he has won a great victory, for he can take us unawares. We are on a war footing, and that war will not end until Christ returns. Only when the Lord Jesus returns from heaven will that war be finally ended. Thank God! But not till then. And this battle of the ages focuses upon God's purpose. It cannot be sufficiently, clearly understood that this whole battle focuses on God's purpose. The salvation of God, of course, is something that the evil one seeks to undermine and blind people to, but it is the purpose of God that is really the focal point. It is because God said, "I will," that the devil says, "no, I will." And there is a great clash of wills over the purpose of God, and we human beings are in the maelstrom of a huge conflict that we rarely understand. However, one day we will be finally forever settled, and only then shall we understand exactly how far and how deep it went. Satan has a vested interest in keeping us blind to God's purpose. If he cannot stop a man or woman being saved, then he will stop them from coming to any understanding of God's purpose. It is obvious; for in war it is essential that we should all be clear as to the supreme objective.

Some of you will remember in the war there was a gentleman called William Joyce that we all nicknamed Lord Haw because he used to haw so much. He always used to say, "Germany calling." He was a traitor, and his whole objective was somehow or other to sow ideas into our minds, to make us fear the might that was against us, to tell us that really there was little on our side. Once the might of the Nazis came, England would crumple like a pack of cards, and he called upon us all to support Germany and to support Hitler because of what was coming. Of course, we all enjoyed it. We all used to listen to Haw-Haw. Even I, as a little boy, remember Haw-Haw because we all laughed so much at the things Lord Haw-Haw said.

But you know, there are a lot of spiritual Haw-Haws, and many Christians are tuned into these spiritual Lord Haw-Haws. All the time they are just saying to us, "You know you are going to go down like a pack of cards when the enemy comes. You will not stand. You do not honestly think the Lord is returning, do you? You do not believe all that rubbish. That is fanatical. That is unbalanced. No! No intelligent person believes that type of rubbish. Then about a hell; there is no such thing as hell. You do not have to bother about the man in your office, the people who live next door to you. Of course not; that is all Middle Age nonsense."

What we do is listen to these "Lord Haws" and somehow or other we start to believe the rubbish that is put out by satanic propaganda and after while we get lulled into sleep. Of course, if the Lord is not really going to come, if it is not really so near, what does it really matter, and this and that? Then we are finished. If these spiritual Lord Haw-Haws can get our minds off the eternal purpose of God and His objective, if by a lot of ideas or some mixed half-truths, and much else, they can just somehow or other get our spiritual minds cluttered up so that we have no room to receive this revelation of God's eternal purpose, they will do it. It is very, very important in war to have a clear understanding of the objective. We want to understand what this war is about. We want to realise that there can be no truck at all with Satan or any evil however small—no truck at all, no compromise. And we also have to understand that we have to see something of God's objective. We have to see not only what Satan is out to get, but we have to see what God is out to get, and that will give us heart in the matter. It is even more important in the day of breakdown and confusion such as ours.

We should also note the apostle Paul's concern that all should fully know and understand this. Here are just a few examples.

Ephesians 1:17: "That the God of our Lord Jesus Christ, the Father of glory, may give unto you a spirit of wisdom and revelation in the knowledge" And this word knowledge is an interesting word. There are two words used for knowledge in the New Testament, and this is a fuller knowledge than the other. "That he may give unto you a spirit of wisdom and revelation in the [full] knowledge of him; having the eyes of your heart enlightened, that ye may know."

In verse 19 you will find the things that Paul wants us to know, and there are few Christians that know them because the eyes of their hearts have not been enlightened.

Philippians 1:9 and we have Paul again praying, and it is interesting to watch the prayer life of the apostle Paul. "And this I pray, that your love may abound yet more and more in knowledge" (And the word again is full knowledge.) "and all discernment."

Colossians 1:9–10 and this is Paul praying again: "For this cause we also, since the day we heard it, do not cease to pray and make request for you, that that ye may be filled with the [full] knowledge of his will in all spiritual wisdom and understanding, to walk worthily of the Lord unto all pleasing, bearing fruit in every good work, and increasing in the [full] knowledge of God." The apostle Paul is very concerned.

Colossians 2:1–2: "For I would have you know how greatly I strive for you, and for them at Laodicea, and for as many as have not seen my face in the flesh," (Mark the word *I strive for you*) "that their hearts may be comforted, they being knit together in love, and unto all riches of the full assurance of understanding, that they may know the mystery of God, even Christ."

This was the burden of Paul's prayer, and I have no doubt in my own mind as to why it was the burden. It was the burden of the Holy Spirit. Later on Paul was to see that this beloved church that he had done so much in bringing into being was to slide away, and what was the beginning of its departure? Blindness! Blindness! People knew that they were saved, and they still believed in their salvation, they still proclaimed the salvation of God right through to the fourth century, but they had lost any real understanding of the eternal purpose of God and His objective. So they were lost in a labyrinth of ways and methods and organization and activity which has been the bugbear of the church from that day to this. The whole thing started here, and Paul's whole prayer was; "Oh, Lord, how could it be preserved? How can it be preserved?" By the eyes of their hearts being enlightened and the full knowledge.

You whom God has been putting His hand upon, you need to understand these things. You really do. It is not just that here we make a lot of it and stress it a lot, you ought to go back to the Lord and get on your knees and say to the Lord: "Lord, I will not rest until I begin to understand what Your purpose is and what Your objective is. Make me a person mastered by Thy purpose."

Three Clues to God's Eternal Purpose

Now we have to ask ourselves very simply: what is that purpose? We have said a lot about the need of knowing it; but what is it? I am not going to say too much about it now. I want to leave that for you to find out yourself, but I am going to give you three very clear clues.

"Christ also loved the church, and gave himself up for it; that he might sanctify it, having cleansed it by the washing of water with the word, that he might present the church to himself a glorious church, not having spot or wrinkle or any such thing; but that it should be holy and without blemish." Ephesians 5:25b–27

That is the calling. If you will pray about that, God will give you a lot of understanding as to what this objective is. We could just describe that as a bride for Christ or God.

> "So then ye are no more strangers and sojourners, but ye are fellow-citizens with the saints, and of the household of God, being built upon the foundation of the apostles and prophets, Christ Jesus himself being the chief corner stone; in whom each several building, fitly framed together, growing into a holy temple in the Lord; in whom ye also are builded together for a habitation of God in the Spirit." Ephesians 2:19–22

We can describe that "a home for God." It is the same thing in another way—a bride for Christ, a home for God.

Ephesians 1:22–23: "And he (God) put all things in subjection under his feet, and gave him to be head over all things to the church, which is his body, the fullness of him that filleth all in all."

I think we could describe that as a body for Christ. In those three phrases you will discover the heart of God's eternal purpose—a bride, a home, a body.

One other thing I think we ought to say about this. I think we should note that everything and everyone has as its objective this matter. Ephesians 4:11–12: "And God gave some apostles; and some, prophets; and some, evangelists; and some, pastors and teachers; for the perfecting of the saints, unto the work of ministering, unto the building up of the body of Christ."

Isn't that interesting? If God makes you an evangelist, what is the objective of your evangelism? It is for the building up of the body of Christ; you are supplying the material. If God makes you a teacher, what is the objective of your teaching? It is for the building up of the body of Christ. If God makes you a prophet or an apostle, what is the objective of your ministry? It is for the building up of the body of Christ. If He makes you a pastor, it is for the building up of the body of Christ. It does not matter who you are, you may be a great apostle, you may be a humble pastor, but in fact, whoever you are and whatever you are, you have the same objective.

Building Up the Church

"So also ye, since ye are zealous of spiritual gifts, seek that ye may abound unto the edifying or building up of the church." 1 Corinthians 14:12

It is the same thing again; it does not matter what spiritual gift you have—tongues, or prophecy, or interpretation, exposition, whatever the gift is—it is to the building up of the church.

"What is it then, brethren? When ye come together, each one hath a psalm, hath a teaching, hath a revelation, hath a tongue, hath an interpretation. Let all things be done unto the building up." Verse 26

Such a simple little word, yet it is the key to everything.

I do not think we can sufficiently stress all these things, but I would like to say that it is not enough to get people saved. We must know to what they have been saved and the clearest straightest ways to secure God's objective. It is even more important if we are called to be fellow-workers with God.

Look in 1 Corinthians 3:9–10 and you will find Paul says, "We are God's fellow-workers: ye are God's husbandry, God's building. I, said Paul, as a master-builder laid the foundation."

Now if you are a master-builder, if you are a fellow-worker with God in this whole matter of God's husbandry, God's tillage, or God's building, it is important for you to know what the plan is. You must know what you are building. Then, the second thing is to see that you are putting good material in. It is important to know that you are putting in good stuff that comes out of spiritual character—Christ in you. But the first thing is to see the plan and the design.

I am going to read to you a little portion from a book, and I suggest that all of you who are thinking about God's service get this book. It is not very well known: *The Secret of His Purpose* by John Kennedy. It is very, very good indeed. It is the only book I know that is written other than brother Watchman Nee's books that comes anywhere near a real understanding of God's purpose. I am going to read just a little portion.

> *"In the light of the prevalent confusion of understanding on the nature of the church, a word must here be said on this subject. Christianity today is a vast conglomeration of so-called churches, some of which are large federations of local groups, diverse in many respects. It contains much which is good, and much also that is evil; those who are truly the people of God and those who are not; rival creeds and rival practices. What relation has all this to what the Scriptures call the church?*

"The fact of historical and organised Christianity, and its obvious difference from the simplicity and spiritual vitality of the churches of the New Testament, has given rise to the widely held distinction between the 'church visible' and 'church invisible.' The 'church visible,' we are told, is all that appears in the world as Christianity with its mixture of good and bad, righteousness and corruption, truth and error, children of God and children of the world. On the other hand, the 'church invisible,' we are told, is the sum total of God's children, those regenerated by the working of the Spirit, whatever their connections in the 'church visible' may be. This distinction, which has no foundation in scripture whatsoever," (Amen.) "has effectively relegated the church to a place of powerlessness in the minds of many of God's people. The 'church visible' is a testimony to man's fallen nature rather than to the glory of God, and the 'church invisible' is a mere theory whose consummation awaits eternity.

"But the church, in the mind of God, transcends the ages. It is a great and powerful fact, not only of eternity but also of time. It is no mere theory. It is a visible reality, and can be known now as surely as it will be in an eternity to come. Our Lord, in that striking series of parables recorded in Matthew 13, likens the church to a pearl. A pearl increases in size with the passage of time, but at whatever stage of its development it may be found it is no less a pearl, a thing of glory and beauty (so is the church). It is true that there are many yet to be added to it, but wherever and whenever it is found it is complete, and an expression of the glory of God.

The layers of nacre which compose a pearl must be together.
Crushed to a powder and scattered to the four winds their
beauty is gone. So it is with the church. The only expression of
the church on earth recognized by the Scriptures is the coming
together of the people of God, the local church,
a visible company of people through whose actual and
practical relationship with the Lord and with one another
the glory of God can be expressed. It is with this local church
that the epistle to the Ephesians deals. The force of this truth
will become more clear in subsequent chapters, but what
has been said will suffice to emphasise that any mention
of the church or assembly in succeeding pages should be
taken to mean not some theoretical company of the elect,
but an actual and visible company of the people of God."

I read that because although we do believe in the church of God which comprises all the saints of all time, for all ages, in the glory and on earth, yet we have got to understand the eternal purpose of God is tied to actual conditions and people down here. It is just here that many of us come unstuck. For if you are going to serve the Lord, you are going to have so much to do with this thing. You have to realise that the eternal purpose of God, the objective of God is to get that eternal purpose secured down here in people who are redeemed of God and brought together and built together so that the material is produced in them for the eternal.

I can only stress all this and leave it with you. But you have to go away to the Lord and ask Him about these things because they are very, very important indeed. This whole question of the eternal purpose of God, in the end, comes down to place. It comes down to geographical localities. It comes down to where God calls you and appoints you, where He places you, and there is no good being mixed up in all these other things. You really have to give yourself to God's purpose in our day and generation.

The Failure of Missions Today

There is a tremendous need of the right kind of missionary today, a tremendous need. I do not suppose there has ever been such need for the right kind of missionary as there is today. The days of pioneer work have largely gone. There is, of course, still place for some pioneer work in different parts of the world, but they have largely gone. In many, many parts of the world there is to some degree now, an indigenous church. As I think most of you know, it is now some one hundred and fifty years since this great era of missionary activity began. For in one generation the gospel has been carried over the whole globe. Two hundred years ago, except for a few scattered outposts of this world, the gospel was an unknown factor. Today, it has been carried to nearly every single part of the world. It is going out from the television, it is going out from the radio, it is going through literature work. The gospel is being carried forth everywhere and being proclaimed, and this is the triumph of missions. That is one side. We have got to underline the fact that thousands, yes, thousands have gone out and laid down their lives, and they will undoubtedly receive their reward. There are some mission stations where it was said in the early days that there were more graves within a few years in the little missionary cemetery than there were missionaries in the station. People died one after another after another to be replaced and die. You have only to read the story of Hudson Taylor and others to realise the sorrow, and the suffering, and the sacrifice.

My dear friends, you and I are just luxury-loving Christians. We are truly Laodicean when it comes to it. We cannot be bothered to go out to the prayer meeting. We prefer our soft chair. We do not like to go out into the streets to meet people. The cost of it is always true. Yet the triumph of missionary endeavor is this: that men and women left everything to live almost near mother Earth, intelligent people, cultured people many of them, people with good background some of them, found it cost them all to leave. This is the triumph of missions.

However, on the other side we must also record the failure of missions. This is the sad side of the picture. For today, we have reproduced all over the world the mistakes, and the mistake of the homeland, not only of this country but the Scandinavian lands and Germany, all those who have been called the homelands, the mother countries of the missions. We have reproduced our own kind. The result is that we have divided up God's children abroad into Baptists, and Anglicans, and Lutherans, and Presbyterians, and Brethren, and Pentecostals, and I do not know what else.

Do you know, when I phoned the World Evangelical Alliance and asked them how many denominations there were in the world, the lady said, "Whew! I could not possibly tell you! Wait, I will go and get the book." She got the book and said, "Oh, there are about thirty-six pages here. I can't possibly count them for you. That was an index of them." This is the failure of missions. We have split up God's people. I cannot say too much about the failure of it. Even where there has been nondenominational work, we have organised the Christians.

We have foisted upon them our own organised type of Christianity, wholly unnatural to them. And then we wonder why on earth they cannot grow with it, and how in many ways they are cramped, restricted, and limited by it. This is the failure of missions.

Now what has happened? God's Holy Spirit is sovereign. Whatever else happens He is absolutely sovereign, and He has raised up men in spite of it all. Of course, unfortunately, there has been a collision with the missions. Now, all over the world we have this unfortunate position that we have great indigenous works of God's Holy Spirit. In China, spread over the whole mainland of China, and wherever there are Chinese-speaking people overseas, we have what is called "Little Flock." In India we have all of the assemblies that are gathered around those staunch men of God headed by Bakht Singh. And elsewhere it is happening in other parts—in the Congo—we have had Pastor David with us. It is happening there and they have had to leave the mission. It is happening everywhere. They are all coming into collision with something that they themselves know to be foreign and alien, not only to them but to God's Word. And now for the first time in the home countries, we are sitting and listening to those who have got something to teach us.

Brother Nee's book, I was told by a man who ought to know, is almost the best seller in America in spiritual books. In fact, it has displaced Henry Drummond's classic on God's great love. God has so arranged these men of different lands, that in spite of the fact that many missions did not like to be on an equality with them, God has done just the opposite and made them superior to us so that now we are the ones who have to sit and listen. And now what has happened? All over the western world people are reading brother Nee's book Concerning Our Missions: The Normal Christian Church Life. We who have sent missionaries to China now have to learn what the church really is because these people have been raised up by God's Holy Spirit, and a new day has dawned in the world. Now you can see the need for the right kind of missionary.

What is needed today are men and women who have seen what God's purpose is, who have really seen what the objective is and can give themselves unreservedly to it, and who can work as equals with the nationals of other countries. No, more than that, they can put themselves at the disposal of the nationals of other countries, and I hate the word, but I am using it for the purpose of distinction. That is what we want, not people who go out thinking they are whites and have something they can teach the blacks and the yellows and all the rest of it. That day is gone. If you want to work in that sphere then do. God is still blessing it; multitudes are still coming to Christ through it. But I want to say this: if you want to be where the candlestick is, and the candlestick of God has been somewhere in every generation, then you have got to see what this eternal purpose of God is, and you have got to give yourself unreservedly to God for that purpose.

When we are in glory, what a joy it will be to find those who in every generation, who worked with what God was doing. They have always been despised and thought to be a bit queer and peculiar. The Puritans were, in their day. They are respectable now, but in their day, everyone had something evil to say about the Puritans. The Quakers, in their day, were despised by everyone, so were the Wesleyans, so were the Brethren. Even Spurgeon said some very unkind things about the Brethren. As for the Pentecostals, we live near enough to them to still hear a lot of very evil things said about them. There is always ground for a certain amount of the criticism, but the whole point is that when you and I are in the glory, we shall find the most amazing harmony, and cohesion, and unity between all of those who have been with what God was doing in their particular generation—always.

So brothers and sisters, especially those of you who have been called to serve the Lord, whatever you do, do not stick to what belongs to another generation. This is truly a natural quality in us all. We are conservative at heart, and we like to hold to something established a hundred years ago. God is called 'I AM that I AM,' and He wants to express Himself to every generation in an absolutely contemporary way. What have we got today? We have some people trying to speak the language of the Reformation, and they still wear the sort of uniform of those days. It was the contemporary language of that day and contemporary uniform of dress, but now it is out of date. How can you reach people today with that kind of dress and that kind of language? And you can come all the way round and find people are still holding to the regulations and the rules that belong to another day. God does not want that. He wants a body.

There is a wonderful thing about my body. Some decades ago it was absolutely new, and now it is absolutely new. I feel a little bit of the passage of time, just a little, but it is still new because my body is organic. It is geared to 1964 not 1936. (I'm not giving anything away.) It is geared to 1964. Now listen carefully. If I get a car of 1934, would it be geared to 1964? No, you cannot do anything about it. It is a car built for 1934; it was brand new then. It was a marvelous model, absolutely contemporary.

Now it is thirty years out of date. My body is not thirty years out of date. It is absolutely contemporary because it is a living thing. God's church is supposed to be just like that. The principle of its being and constitution is that it can be absolutely contemporary at any given time to the world of its day. But because we do not understand God's purpose, we do not understand the nature of what we are in, all the time we are crystallising it, cramping it, restricting it so that God cannot move. And so you have these great successive movements of God's Holy Spirit when it is absolutely fresh in that day.

The Great Need

I only want to say to you that there is a very, very great need therefore for men and women who have seen something of what God wants. There is still a place for pioneers. There is still a place for that if God has so called you, but the greatest need today is for men whom God has done something in, and who have seen so clearly that they can go out to help, go out to lead, to steer, to share. This is the great need, and it is this that you and others ought to ask God about. You cannot get this, and I say this advisedly, in any Bible college, important sometimes as Bible College training is. You cannot get it in any course of lectures. You can only get this by revelation, by the eyes of your heart being enlightened by the Holy Spirit of God, and you not only seeing it, but being brought into it. You will never get it unless you start to pray. For those who seek God, they shall find Him, not only in a first way, primary way, initial way, but in every other way, whatever stage you are in. You will never come into more of the Lord unless you seek Him. God never hands out blessings in a cheap way. He watches, He waits, and He gives us grace to seek Him until finally He answers us and enlightens us. But this is the need of our day.

Let me close by saying this. I do not suppose that in the whole history of the world, there have ever been more missionaries than there are on this planet tonight. And I do not suppose there have ever been more missionary societies or missionary works of one kind or another—radio, film work, literature work as well as evangelistic work, medical work, and much else. And yet, I think you all are aware we are losing ground. Everywhere over the whole world we are losing ground. In the first century it all began with one hundred and twenty in an upper room. They had never been to a Bible college. In one sense, they had very little real training. The only training they had was by being with the Master for three years, and even then they hopelessly misunderstood Him. Yet when the Holy Spirit of God came that day, that hundred and twenty went out, and in one generation they had evangelised the whole of the Roman Empire. And we believe that they had probably even taken the gospel to Britain, and it is certain they had taken the gospel to India. Within a century the gospel had gotten to China with the Nestorians. They did something that we have not been able to do.

It was not that they made the mistake we made in the beginning, for everywhere over the whole inhabited world the church came into being. It took time for the evil one to counteract it, to overcome it, to divide it and finally to submerge it. But you know there was a secret and I believe the secret was this: they knew the cross, they knew the Spirit, and they knew the purpose of God. It was within them, and they went out. I think of men like Timothy. Where did he learn these things? Well, Paul used to take him around with him and that was how he learned those things. He was like an apprentice, for want of a better word, and he watched Paul and he did a lot of odd jobs. Gradually, he learned not only by instruction, by listening, but also by observation.

I think you and I have to understand today that we need to be brought into a new place altogether with the Lord, and we want to see something happen in our day and generation as great as anything that has happened before, if not greater. It is not that we want some place; we want it for the glory of the Lamb. This old world cannot go on much longer like this. We want to bring back the Lord, and the only way the Lord can be brought back is by this next step being taken. There is a further step. It may be the last step.

Latourette, in his *A History of the Expansion of Christianity* has pointed out that there is a very apparent ebb and flow in church history. There is a movement of the Spirit that takes something up, and something is recovered, that had been lost after Pentecost, and then there is the end. Then there is another move of the Spirit, and it takes it up and something else is recovered, and then there is the end. So it was with the Puritans, the Quakers, the Wesleyans, the Brethren, the Pentecostals; each flow takes us farther up the shore. And he points out that in the end it is probable that there will be one last great flow of the Spirit of God which will carry us right up the shore, and at that point the Lamb will come and carry us right into the kingdom.

I do not know where we are. I would not like to say we are at that last one; I have my own strong feelings about it. To be absolutely safe, I will say there is another step needed, and it is that for which we pray. We do believe we see the first signs in this country and elsewhere of something beginning to happen. We believe the tide is turning. Something is happening. Men and women in different denominations are being quickened. Strange things are on the move which betoken something supernatural, something beyond us that God is doing. We want to be in it.

Now listen, when that flow comes, there is always the possibility of you being carried with the flow without understanding what is happening. We need men and women who know, and when the flow comes, when the move comes, they know what it is about. It is not that they are mastering it; it is mastering them, but they have discernment, they have wisdom, they can distinguish, and in the right way they can channel the flow. Oh, may God help us so to understand! It is a fact in church history that within one generation of every move of the Holy Spirit the rot has set in. May God help us then in our day and help those of you who are seeking the Lord in this way to be prepared. Seek the Lord earnestly that He may enlighten the eyes of your heart that you might know.

3.
Abiding

We have been having some special studies for those who have responded to the Lord's challenge and committed yourselves to Him ready to go anywhere that He should direct you. There is a sense in which every one of us are servants of the Lord and wherever God has appointed us to be, we serve Him there in the Spirit as His witnesses. Yet there is a sense in which some are called in a peculiar way into God's work, and it is those we are addressing, although of course what we are saying has meaning for every single one of us.

We have already dealt with one or two matters, those characteristics that God looks for in those who would serve Him. We have already spoken of an utter devotion to Christ leading to worship, to service, and to testimony. The second characteristic God looks for is an implicit faith in God and in His Word. Last time we dealt with that characteristic which we have entitled: a clear understanding of God's purpose and objective.

Now I want to add another characteristic—an ever increasing experience of all that God has provided for us in and through Christ. In Colossians 2:9–10 it says: "For in him (Christ) dwelleth all the fullness of the Godhead bodily, and in him, ye are made full, who is the head of all principality and power."

What a word for those who would serve the Lord! "For in Christ dwelleth all the fullness of the Godhead bodily, and in him, ye are made full, or complete, who is the head of all principality and power"—an ever increasing experience of all that God has provided for us in and through Christ. The path of the just should be as a shining light which shines more and more unto the perfect day. It is not always so. I am afraid that Christendom is littered with people who started on the road and somehow or other have gotten sidetracked. What happened to Lot's wife has happened again and again and again in Christian circles. All along the way you can see those who have stopped, those who have become static in their Christian life or have gotten off into side paths, into side pastures and settled down. God looks for, as a characteristic in those who would serve Him, an ever-increasing experience—not just a blessing you had so many years ago—but an ever-increasing, up-to-date experience of all that He has provided for us in and through Christ.

Complete Provision in Christ

God has provided completely everything necessary for the Christian life and for the church in Christ. He has provided everything! He has provided all that is necessary for the initial stage of the Christian life, that is, new birth; all we have to do is accept it. He has made every provision for going on and for living the Christian life, for its development, for the reproducing of the character and nature of Christ. He has made all provision that is necessary for our being transformed from glory to glory, and He has made all the provision for our being made perfect in the end. Now believe it or believe it not, God has made complete provision for all this that we may be transformed and conformed until at last we stand before God without spot or blemish or any such thing. This is a wonderful subject to deal with, to recognise that God has made provision like this.

God has also provided completely everything necessary for the church, not only for its being founded and planted, its being brought to birth, but its development, for all its gifts, its functions, and its service. He has made provision for its triumphs, its perseverance, its increase, its multiplication. God has made complete provision. There is not one single thing that God has not forethought. In His foreknowledge He has provided for every possible emergency, both in the personal believer's life and in the church's life. It is all completely provided in Christ, and that is the only condition.

Now, if you are looking outside of Christ, you will look until kingdom come but you will find no provision. You will become more and more tired, more and more weary, more and more unhappy, more and more disappointed and disillusioned, for you are looking in the wrong place. God has made all provision in Christ. And if the church starts to look outside of Christ for its power, for its influence, for its organisation, for its gifts and service and all the rest of it, then it will bewail its condition. It may have a million servants, it may have a thousand and one great campaigns, but it will still bewail its condition, for it will discover that all that it is seeking to do, all of the resources it is seeking to draw upon will not somehow or other bring it into what it sees in the New Testament as its condition and character. This is very important.

Let's put it another way because we must be absolutely clear on this matter. There is no point in you who are going to serve the Lord getting muddled or confused here. We are going to take a little bit of time and just absolutely underline this. Let's put it the other way round so it becomes even clearer. There is nothing essential to the believer or to the church which is not provided in Christ. That is as simple as we can put it. There is nothing essential to the believer, to you or me, necessary to our going on to our birth spiritually or development, or perfection, our triumphing personally, nothing that is not provided by God in Christ and the same with the church. It is all there. All is ours in Him and given to us with Him. When God gave us Christ, He gave with Him everything we could possibly need. If we had a life down here that stretched for a million years, we still would not come to the end of what God has provided in Christ—immeasurable, inexhaustible power and life is in Christ.

Romans 8:32: "He that spared not his own Son, but delivered him up for us all, how shall he not also with him freely give us all things?" When God has given Christ, then He has given everything. Therefore, all of this is lavished upon us with Him.

In Christ

I Corinthians 1:30: "But of him are ye in Christ Jesus, who was made unto us wisdom from God, and righteousness and sanctification, and redemption: that, according as it is written, He that glorieth, let him glory in the Lord."

Will you notice two things? First, of him, of God are ye in Christ Jesus. God has put us in Christ Jesus, and when we are in Christ Jesus we find that God has made Jesus to be righteousness, sanctification, and redemption. These three are described as the wisdom of God, and they cover the whole Christian life—justification, sanctification, glorification—all is covered. Christ is made to us completely all that we need.

That their hearts may be comforted, they being knit
together in love, and unto all riches of the full assurance
of understanding, that they may know the mystery
of God, even Christ, in whom are all the treasures of
wisdom and knowledge hidden. (Colossians 2:2-3)

Will you notice that it says, "... all the treasures of wisdom and knowledge are hidden"? God has placed all the treasures of wisdom and knowledge in Christ.

Blessed be the God and Father of our Lord Jesus Christ,
who hath blessed us with every spiritual blessing in
the heavenly places in Christ. (Ephesians 1:3)

This ought to raise some questions for a lot of us as we go on. Will you notice first the tense: "... who hath blessed us with every spiritual blessing"? Secondly, will you notice it is "... every spiritual blessing"? If every spiritual blessing is already in Christ for us, it is a tremendous thing when you think about it. What blessing do you want? There are people who talk about second blessings and there is evidently therefore a first blessing. And there are many other blessings, all kinds of things that we could call blessings. Every blessing that God has given us is in Christ.

And my God shall supply every need of yours according
to his riches in glory in Christ Jesus. (Philippians 4:19)

Every need of yours is met according to His riches in glory. Now that is the condition—according to His riches in glory in Christ Jesus.

John 16:33 is just one of a large number of references that deal with special qualities or special virtues that the Lord gives to us. This one has to do with peace. "These things have I spoken unto you, that in me ye may have peace. In the world ye have tribulation: but be of good cheer I have overcome the world."

That is very wonderful really. The Lord Jesus said, "In me you have peace," and the idea of the peace here is triumph; it is peace that comes through a war being successfully concluded. "I have overcome the world. In me you have peace; in the world you have tribulation." But there is a sense in which we should know both things at the same time. In Christ we should have perfect peace, but all the time we are in the world we have tribulation. Of course, it stands to reason that if you are a Christian and you are not centering in Christ, then you are going to have more tribulation than peace. The peace is there for you in Christ. So the more you get into Christ, the more peace you will know.

In Romans 8:37 after this tremendous catalogue of things, Paul said, "And yet, in spite of all, overwhelming victory is ours through Him who loved us" (NEB). In spite of all, overwhelming victory is ours through Him who loved us.

Abiding in Christ

If all is ours in Christ and if we are to have an ever-increasing experience of Him, we have got to learn the secret of abiding in Him. That is the key to everything. Do you know that the key to stability, the key to spiritual poise and balance is this matter of abiding in Christ? I am convinced of it, and more and more convinced of it that until a person learns through faith to remain in Christ, they can be knocked all over the place. One day they are this, the next day they are that. We can be up and we can be down, but when we are rooted in Christ, we can go up and down, but there is a balance in spite of it all. We are abiding in the Lord.

John 6:56: "He that eateth my flesh and drinketh my blood abideth in me, and I in him." The way that you come to abide in Christ is by receiving the Lord. The way you remain in Christ is to open up to Him all the time. It is so simple. How do you eat and drink? Every day you have set times when you have a little meal or even in between nibble takings, but you are taking something and you are eating; you are receiving it into yourself. You desire it; you appreciate it, and you appropriate it. You take it and you make it your own, both for food and for liquid. You eat and you drink. "He that eateth my flesh and drinketh my blood abideth in me and I in him." How do we stay in Christ? By continually opening our hearts to Him. How do we do that? The same way we began. When we first started, we said, "Lord Jesus, I open my heart to Thee; I receive Thee." That moment I entered into Christ and Christ entered into me. Although in one sense I said, "I receive You," in fact, God said, "No, I place you in Christ and I place Christ in you." You step into Christ and Christ steps into you the moment you receive Him. It is so simple really how to go on. Every moment when you are in, open your heart and say, "Lord Jesus, I take more of You." That is all you have to do. That is how you feed on the Lord. It is simply childlike. Just say, "Lord Jesus, I take more of You." Every time you do that you are triumphing in a strange way because you are taking more of Christ, and it seems so silly; it seems so foolish. What can it do? But in a strange way, it is the way through because you are abiding.

I have learned it. Brother Nee was the first one to teach me of the secret. I had read much about it through Andrew Murray and I understood quite a lot from him, but it was brother Nee who, when I first asked him a question about ministry, said, "My dear brother, all you have to do is get on your knees and say, 'Lord, I cannot give anything of life to these people, but I open my heart and I take more of Thee.' Every time you do that, there will be life." So I proved it; that is all I can say. I just simply proved it. When you feel dead, you feel under, all you have to say is, "Lord Jesus, I take more of Thee." It is so simple. You are feeding on the Lord. The spirit in you is eating His flesh; your spirit is drinking His blood, and you are abiding in Him, and He is abiding in you.

Of course, there are many other ways. We say we do it through prayer, that is the simplest form of prayer: "Lord Jesus, I receive more of Thee; I open my heart and take more of Thee by faith." That is prayer. Of course it comes through God's Word. When you are chewing over God's Word, when you have taken God's Word and it is in your heart. You think about it. You do not understand it, but you ask the Lord for more of Himself so you can understand His Word.

John 15 is a step further. John chapter 6 tells us how to begin and how to continue. John 15 is service in the church; the vine is Christ, the church. Verse 4–7: "Abide in me, and I in you. As the branch cannot bear fruit of itself, except it abide in the vine; so neither can ye, except ye abide in me. I am the vine, ye are the branches: He that abideth in me, and I in him, the same beareth much fruit: for apart from me ye can do nothing. If a man abide not in me, he is cast forth as a branch, and is withered; and they gather them, and cast them into the fire, and they are burned. If ye abide in me, and my words abide in you, ask whatsoever ye will, and it shall be done unto you."

This is a very interesting sidelight on prayer. If we are abiding in Christ, and God's Word, Christ, is abiding in us, then we can ask whatsoever we will and it shall be given to us. Abiding is the key. God hears prayer when we are abiding in Christ. That is what we do when we say, "in the name of Jesus." Really, all I am saying is: "I am abiding in Christ." That is why I pray in the name of the Lord Jesus.

This word abide means "to dwell, to remain, and to continue." The best way we can see and understand it is by reading Acts 27:27–31 in the New English Bible because I think it is easier to get the point. "The fourteenth night came and we were still drifting in the sea of Adria. In the middle of the night the sailors felt that land was getting nearer. They sounded and found twenty fathoms. Sounding again after a short interval they found fifteen fathoms, and fearing that we might be cast ashore on a rugged coast they dropped four anchors from the stem, and prayed for daylight to come. The sailors tried to abandon ship; they had already lowered the ship's boat, pretending they were going to lay out anchors from the bows, when Paul said to the centurion and the soldiers, 'Unless these men stay on board you can none of you come off safely.'"

Now, "stay on board" is abide. In the AV it is abide. Here is the word: stay on board. It is so simple. We have a beautiful illustration: "stay on board" and you are safe. There is a great storm raging and you are getting so frightened about it. You think, "Oh, dear, I am going to go down. Something terrible is going to happen. I had better try and meet this." So you get into a little boat because you think if you could get to the coastline you would be safe. You must be sensible. When these great big spiritual storms come, somehow or other you have to meet them with common sense, haven't you? But you see the answer is to abide; that is the secret.

This is not so childish as it may seem. Right through the Old Testament this is the lesson that many of the patriarchs and others had to learn. God told Abraham to abide in the Promised Land,

and then a famine came. Now we might say, "No famine should come if you are in the center of God's will," but a famine did come, and Abraham was in the center of God's will. And Abraham said, "We have a great retinue of servants, we have flocks and herds, and the simplest, most common sensical thing we can do is go down into Egypt where there is plenty. The Lord knows we won't stay in Egypt. We will just go down into Egypt and stay a little while, and as soon as things are better we will come back. Surely the Lord wants us to do that."

But you see, the moment Abraham stepped out of the Promised Land and went down into Egypt, he was out of Christ, as it were, and he got himself into a great mess. The interesting thing is that when he came back to the land, he had to go right back to the very point from which he had departed before he could go on with the Lord. It is only a little lesson, but this question of abiding is simple but profound. It is the key to the whole Christian life.

You and I have got to remain where God has placed us. God has placed us in Christ and we have got to learn to abide there. The whole Christian life and the church is bound up and explained in two things—our being in Christ and Christ being in us. Do you know that is the Christian life? I have the Christian life because God has placed me in Christ and He has placed Christ in me. That is the Christian life. Do you know that we are the church simply because all of us have been placed in one Christ and one Christ has been placed in all of us? If we would only learn to abide in Christ we would find the secret both of the Christian life and of the church.

Christ Abiding in Me

What is the secret? The secret is Christ. If you abide in Christ you will find that Christ is in you. That is the secret. First, get into the sphere and then you will find the power. Get into Christ and then you will find that Christ is in you. It is the same with the church. I want to underline this first of all. God has made complete provision for us both personally and corporately in Christ. God, through new birth and our faith in the Lord Jesus, has placed us in Christ. Now the secret is abide. For as I abide in Christ, Christ abides in me. That is the secret.

The New English Bible has a most remarkable rendering in Colossians 2:6–7. "Therefore since Jesus was delivered to you as Christ and Lord, live your lives in union with Him. Be rooted in Him, be built in Him, be consolidated by the faith you were taught. Let your heart overflow with thankfulness. Be on your guard; do not let your minds be captured by hollow and delusive speculations, based on the traditions of man-made teaching and centered on the elemental spirits of the world and not on Christ."

The thing I want to note here is that just as we received Christ Jesus the Lord, so we ought to walk in Him. We are to be rooted and builded up in Him and established by our faith. Faith is the key again. You have to remain where God has placed you so that you can be rooted and built. In other words, do not move. It is so simple. Stay where you have been placed and get rooted and built up, established by your faith in Him.

The devil's most immediate and direct objective in us all is to get us out of Christ. He can do it in a thousand ways, and usually through our ignorance of his devices, he seems to win. He can suggest that we are unworthy. He can bring up past sins. He can bring up some present failure and immediately, as we start to dwell on it, gradually he sort of teases us almost and entices us out of Christ until we are out without Christ. His whole objective is to practically divorce us from Christ. He knows he cannot do it officially and legally, but in practical experience he can divorce us from Christ. We are true Christians, saved through the blood of the Lamb, but we have no experience whatsoever of Christ. It is all stopped, for we have stepped out of Him and a divorce has taken place. This is exactly what Colossians is about; people have gone back by stepping out of Christ.

Stand and Withstand

In Ephesians 6:10–11, 13–14a this battle is exactly what is described there: "Finally, be strong in the Lord." (Mark this: *in the Lord*.) "and in the strength of his might. Put on the whole armor of God," (I understand that is Christ. We are to be strong in the Lord and in the strength of His might.) "that ye may be able to stand against the wiles of the devil...Wherefore take up the whole armor of God, that ye may be able to withstand in the evil day, and, having done all, to stand. Stand therefore ..."

It is quite remarkable that this is all to do with abiding. God has put us in Christ and our whole job is to stand. Why stand? What is the idea of standing? The whole point of the devil is to move us out of Christ and Paul says whatever happens in the battle, stand, withstand, and having done everything, stand. Don't take a step forward, don't take a step back, just stand. Don't let the devil get you out. Don't let him say, "Come out, come on, come on. You can take Christ, can't you, to come out?" Just stand. Don't go back, don't go forward. Stand.

The battle there is one of getting us outside of Christ. This matter of being in Christ is all-important, and abiding in Him is the key. How do you abide in Him? As I said, it is by simple faith continually opening your heart to receive more of the Lord.

In this connection, let's note carefully that it has all been provided through the cross and the Spirit, that is, through Calvary and Pentecost. It has. Have you noted that all the tenses in these verses that we first read are in the past? It is all ours. God has provided it. "Blessed with every spiritual blessing in heavenly places in Christ." It is ours the moment we put our trust in Christ.

Let me illustrate. Have you ever read in the paper of someone dying and leaving a large sum of money? They had young relatives, either young children or a young nephew or niece. The paper says they had put in their will that their money was to be put in trust until so and so had reached the age of twenty-one or twenty-two or maybe thirty. Some people so distrust their children that it is not until forty. But the will says that at such and such an age this whole fortune, whatever it is will become theirs practically.

Now take note: at Calvary and Pentecost God gave us a spiritual fortune. He provided for us every single thing you and I will ever need, and it was all held in trust until the day you and I were born of God. The moment you and I were born of God's spirit we inherited, in one sense. We came into it; it was ours. The provision was ours, but it was held in trust. It is all past. God gave it to us at Calvary and Pentecost. It is all there, but it is all held in trust. When you and I simply put our faith in the Lord Jesus Christ, and are born of the Spirit, in that moment God says it is ours.

You can start using it now. You are only a babe to begin with and you will not need so much to begin with, but it is all yours. Just get on with it and use as much as you can. We can never overstress this fact that it is ours at spiritual birth because of Calvary and Pentecost. I do not think it can be stressed enough. Everything is ours. We do not have to go looking for it. It is ours. It has been given to us at Calvary and Pentecost. They were the two great movements of God in this matter of the giving to us everything that is necessary to the Christian life and the church.

Now we come to the practical problem. If it is true that all is ours, everything is ours in Christ, why the spiritual poverty in so many of us, in fact, the majority of us? Why the defeat? Why the failure? Why the absence of fullness? the weakness? the emptiness? the shallowness? We have to face the simple fact that although all has been provided for us in Christ, few live in the full good and enjoyment of it. Let me ask you: I wonder how many of us are actually living in the full good and enjoyment of everything that is ours in Christ. Are you? Are you abiding? Have you even learned the first simple secret of this matter of the Christian life and the church of abiding? I wonder if I am right in saying that I suspect that nearly ninety-nine percent of us, or higher, are not in fact anywhere near living in the full good and enjoyment of it. Yet God has made provision that we should live in the full good of it. It is no good blaming it on God. It is no good saying it is the times in which we live. God has made the provision for us, and it is all in the past. It is done. Calvary and Pentecost are sufficient for it. It is sufficient for overcoming hell; quite sufficient. We have no excuse. Now why the discrepancy?

Well, I think we have to put it very simply—because it must be appropriated; that is why. It must be appropriated.

Possessing Our Possession

Joshua 1:4–6: "From the wilderness, and this Lebanon, even unto the great river, the river Euphrates, all the land of the Hittites, and unto the great sea toward the going down of the sun, shall be your border. There shall not any man be able to stand before thee all the days of thy life: as I was with Moses, so I will be with thee; I will not fail thee, nor forsake thee. Be strong and of good courage; for thou shalt cause this people to inherit the land which I sware unto their fathers to give them."

Now if we were to stop there, that is what most of us have got. We have a Bible, we have a great salvation, we have a greater God, we have a tremendous promise, and yet there is a secret. Verse 3: "Every place that the sole of your foot shall tread upon, to you have I given it, as I spake unto Moses."

In other words, the wilderness would never be able to stand before him. All of this great territory from the Mediterranean to the Euphrates, from the Nile up beyond Syria, is yours. No one will be able to stand before you, but the key to it all is, as it were, traversing or taking it for God. The Lord will do everything, but you have to put your foot down. It is just as if we were to say to Joshua: "Joshua, everything is yours. Everything is yours, Joshua. Canaan is yours, and Mesopotamia is yours, and Babylon is yours, and Egypt is yours. All is yours, Joshua. And what's more Joshua, God has made provision for you in every way. He will not only give it to you, but you will be able to get all the wealth out of it, you will be able to live in it, and be established in it all." Then we could say, "Listen to this, Joshua: 'There is not one single person, whoever it is, however great the pharaoh of Egypt may be or the emperor of Babylon or Assyria, not one of them will be able to stand before you. The moment you step in, they will collapse. It is just as simple as that, Joshua. It is all yours."

Then supposing Joshua had sat down on the other side of the river Jordan and waited, like most of us do. Oh, he used to sing lovely songs about the whole land from the Nile to the Euphrates being his. He used to sing wonderful songs praising the Lord that all the enemies of God would be smitten down and destroyed. He sang wonderful songs and had wonderful prayer meetings about the purpose of God being to establish a people in this wonderful land that He was giving them. And then one day he began to wake up. Perhaps some of the younger ones began to prod him and say to him: "Well, Joshua, we have been here for years, and we have not gone over into the land, and nothing has happened. Far from having it from the Nile to the river Euphrates, we are still living in tents. We just have a little tiny area which is ours in the desert."

The key to the whole thing is this: Joshua had to step over that Jordan and see it split into two. It is the only way we will get over the Jordan. If he had said, "Now, God send down an angel and split the water, and when we see that happen, we will go over in triumph." The Lord would never have done it. Joshua had to tell the priests: "Go forward and step into the water." The moment the soles of their feet touched the water it split into two and the people went over.

The moment the soles of their feet went around Jericho again and again and again without one single word, the seventh time on the seventh day the walls fell down. It was the soles of their feet that was the key to it all. Someone read to us the other Sunday morning that C. T. Studd said, "Thank God, I have big feet." It is really a question of possessing. It is such a simple secret.

Do you think Joshua felt marvellous as he watched those priests going down to the waters of Jordan's flood tide? Don't you think he felt butterflies in his stomach and just wondered, "Well, aren't we a lot of fools? Just look at us; those poor weak men going down to the water to put their feet on it! What a silly thing to do!" What do you think the people called down from the battlements of Jericho? One of the most wonderful ramifications in the whole land was the fort that protected the path into the Promised Land. What do you think the people said as they saw this crowd of idiots, in their eyes, going round and round the walls blowing trumpets on the last day and silent the other days? They must have thought, what a crowd of fools!

You know, this is just where our faith fails. You only have to have a snicker from the world, and even worse, you only have to have a snicker from Christians, and your faith collapses. You do not want to be silly. You do not want to look a fool. You do not want to make any advances. Everyone is frightened of everyone else. If they will all jump together, it's all right, but everyone is frightened otherwise. The only way the thing can be possessed is by the soles of our feet. We have to go down and take it. And the devil will see to it that in one way or another, we are all waylaid. It can be difficult husbands, or difficult wives, or difficult children, or difficult circumstances, or it can be health, or many other things. And the devil only has to raise these things. At the beginning there may be a real case for it, but it becomes counterfeit after a while. We take it all and get frightened of it, and we retreat. The real secret is to put our feet down and claim the thing for God and what is of the devil disappears. What is absolutely, genuinely physical or genuinely belonging to circumstances remains until the Lord wonderfully overcomes them or changes us. But oh, for this secret!

Examples of Appropriating

What does it mean to appropriate, really? Someone might say, "It is a very hard word for me to understand." Let me illustrate: Look here, I am thirsty. And here on this table there has been provided a decanter full of water and a glass. It is full provision for a thirsty speaker. Supposing I were to say to you, "I am getting more and more thirsty, and I do not know what is going to happen, but I must go on." Finally my throat dries up, and I cannot speak anymore. You would say, "What is wrong with you? There is a whole decanter full of water on the table." But I have not seen it. If I have not seen it and I do not appreciate that there is water for my thirsty throat and lips, I cannot do anything about it because I do not see it. So I suffer. But the moment I see the water, hallelujah! I take the glass and the decanter and I appropriate it. I have appropriated the water. Isn't that a simple thing?!

What does it mean to appropriate Christ? God has made all provision for your need. All you have to do is say, "Lord, I take Thee. I appropriate what is mine, and I take it by faith." That is appropriation. We may be in Christ, Christ may be in us, we may be abiding in Him, but we need our eyes to be opened to see what is ours in Him. Do you realise that you can be in Christ and be blind? You can be in Christ and Christ may be in you, and you may even have learned to abide there by faith, but the eyes of your heart are not open. So you see Him as your salvation, but you may not see Him as your life. And you will say to me one day, "God has provided Christ as my life." And immediately, just like I am taking that glass of water, you take Christ as your life; you have the secret. You can do that with all kinds of things whatever your need is.

Let me illustrate it again. Supposing tomorrow morning I find a letter awaiting me to tell me that 200,000 pounds has been left to me by a dear old aunt somewhere or other that I never knew existed. And she has made it all over to me. I open a bank account and put the 200,000 pounds in, and I am given a chequebook. Now, what happens if I have a fortune in the bank? The first thing is I have to appreciate it. I have to appreciate the extent of my fortune. Supposing I need a Rolls and I think I have only 500 pounds in the bank. That is no good, is it? I cannot get a Rolls for 500 pounds. But supposing I have 200,000 pounds in the bank, then I can get a Rolls. I take my chequebook and I write out a check for 10,000 pounds and I have my Rolls. I have appropriated what is mine in the bank and I have met the need.

How are you and I to live in Christ? How are we to exploit and appropriate the provision which is ours? It is all there for us. God has given us the chequebook. We simply have to appreciate what is ours. Most of us have a horrible idea that the Lord Jesus is very stingy with us in particular. "Lance has got a spiritual fortune in heaven's bank, but I have just a few hundred. Of course, he can do this and he can do that, but I can't." However, God has made no distinction. He has given us all a fortune in Christ. It is for every one of us. The thing is you have got to appreciate it. If you do not inwardly see what you have in the bank and appreciate it, you will never start using it. The moment you inwardly see what Christ can be to you, what He is, what God has made Him to be for you and then you begin to appreciate the extent of His fullness, then you will start to come and draw on it. And you do not need to worry about how much you draw from the Lord Jesus; you can go on and go on and go on. It is all there.

Calvary and Pentecost

All that God has provided in Christ is made over to us in a four-fold way through Calvary and Pentecost. Both these main peaks of our full salvation are two-sided. The work of the cross is two-fold and the work of the Spirit is two-fold. We can say that our salvation is four-fold or four square, if you like. I think this can be helpful, although we cannot be clinical about our salvation. If we break it up a little, it may help us to understand in what area of this great salvation we are lacking. This is what it has always felt to me anyway. Just to understand we have a great salvation is one thing, but to analyze and break it up a little, you may suddenly discover the area of your weakness. Now you have to ask the Lord to open your eyes there so that you can see.

There are two main peaks in the work of our redemption. There is Calvary and there is Pentecost. Calvary is two-fold or two-sided and Pentecost is two-fold; its work is two-fold or two-sided.

It is as simple as that. There are these four points. Christ is our full salvation. "Ye are complete in Him."

First of all, through Calvary we are justified. That is one side of the work of Calvary at the cross and it is absolutely essential. The second side of the work of Calvary is that we are crucified. That is the other side of the work of the cross. Pentecost also has two sides. The first side of Pentecost, the work of the Spirit, is that we are indwelt. The second side is that we are empowered.

Now you will see straightaway that we have an absolutely full salvation. That is all God's provision for us. Every single thing you require is found somewhere in these two peaks. Everything. There is not one thing that is not found somewhere in this full salvation. Do you want peace? Do you want love? Do you want patience? Do you want forbearance? Do you want joy? A lot of it is bound up with the indwelling of the Holy Spirit. Do you want to be free from yourself? Free from all its power and its energy? Then you have to know something of the cross, being crucified with Christ. Do you want to be released from your conscience? Do you want to know something of pardon and forgiveness and the peace and joy that comes with it? It is in the being justified. Do you need to know what it is to be lifted right above one's self? To be able, really, to serve the Lord in an almost supernatural way? Then you have to know the empowerment of the Lord, the anointing of God.

One side of the work of our salvation, we can say is in Christ. We are justified in Christ and we are crucified in Christ. Then, it is very wonderful to see that it is Christ within. We are indwelt by the Spirit of Christ and empowered by the Spirit of Christ.

If we are children of God, all of us must have some experience of the first part of the work of the cross. Every single one of us has some experience of justification. Otherwise, we could not be children of God. Even so, I am amazed at what a weak experience it is so often in those of us who know the Lord. The question of justification is not so much belonging to infancy; it is absolutely foundational to everything. But this is the point. I have said that everything is ours in Christ. All of us must have an experience of this first side of Calvary, but we can stop there. Though we have pardon, and though we have forgiveness, and though we have the remission of our sins, and though we know Christ as our righteousness, our salvation, we are absolutely ignorant of anything more. It is rather like living life with only one lung. You can get through, but for a good, full, strong life you need two good lungs. And many Christians are living as it were, on one lung and half an experience. They know what it is to be saved, they know what it is to have taken the blood of Christ for their sins, but there is this other side.

Although we may have had an experience of being justified we can stop there. Of these four peaks, we can have three of them, or two of them, or we may have only one, the first one. Someone may say to me, "Do you really mean to tell me that someone can be justified and know what it is to be empowered without being crucified?"

The strange thing is that it is possible. You just cannot be clinical with spiritual experiences. It is a most remarkable thing. In this question of baptism of the Spirit, people can get baptized in the Spirit and because they do not know anything about being crucified with Christ they can get into the most fearful excesses.

They go all over the place, shooting around, doing stupid things because they have become so bold and so empowered, but they are not broken. There is something of God in them, but they are not broken. Do you understand? It is most interesting. You can know what it is to be crucified, and you can know what it is to be indwelt. In this sense you have a real knowledge of the Lord, but you are absolutely filled with fear because you have no experience of the empowering of the Holy Spirit. Every time you come to pray, you are so full of fear you do not know what to do. That should not be. Every time you try to speak to someone about the Lord in the office, you just do not know what to do. You feel really sick. I have Christians come to me and say, "I really felt sick. I felt I had to go out." Is there anything less New Testament? You do not hear of Peter sort of running out for a breath of fresh air because he felt so sick. There is something wrong.

When the Holy Spirit empowered them, all the bolts on the door came off; the doors were opened and out they went. But before that, where were they? Although they knew a risen Christ, though they knew what it was to be justified, yet they were frightened men in an upper room, frightened because of fear of the Jews. But the moment the Spirit came, out they went and stood up and preached to that crowd. Then the rulers said to Peter a little later, "We forbid you to speak in this Name," and Peter stood up and said, "I am sorry I cannot accept that. I will go on speaking in the Name." They put him in prison and he was not the least bit afraid. James, they took out and executed; Peter was delivered by an angel. They took it all so calmly. These were ordinary men like us. They were as frightened as us; they were as fearful beings as us. In fact, I can well imagine that because they did not have a kind of university education, they would have been terribly frightened to speak before many of those cultured men in the temple on the day of Pentecost. But something so marvellous happened that even people who were watching said, "These men must be drunk to speak like this." This is our four-fold salvation.

Now, what I want to ask you is this: Where have you stopped? If you have had an experience of justification, do you know anything about the cross? Do you know anything about the indwelling Holy Spirit? Do you know anything about the baptism of the Holy Spirit? Never let theology, so-called, stop you from seeking more of Christ. Theology in itself, truth in itself can become a curse when it becomes bondage. Because we all say, "It is all ours in Christ; the moment we were saved it was ours," then there comes this bondage: "You must not ask. You must not inquire. You must not seek. It's ours; it's ours." It is absolutely true! It is ours, but we have to possess it. We have to put the soles of our feet down and say, "Lord, this which You have done, this which You have given, this which You have provided has to become mine corporately and personally." Until you and I do that, we will not experience it.

It is faith that does it. It is not that you feel better, or you feel so good that you say, "Dear brother, I do believe I am crucified. I really do believe I am crucified. I have been feeling better and better this week, and I think at any moment now I am going to pass into the experience." My dear friend, it will never come like that. Never! You will never go around and say, "I feel so wonderful; I felt so marvellous this last week that I do believe I am on the verge of an experience of the indwelling of the Holy Spirit." You will never feel it like that, not in your life. I reckon that's something you have eaten or something that belongs to you temperamentally. You are just "up," that's all. But when you have seen it, you can be absolutely down and yet by faith you can step into it. The eyes of your heart have been enlightened, and you have stepped into it. From that moment it becomes yours.

However, let me say this: we cannot be clinical in our approach to spiritual things. The great need is to be in the good of all that God has provided for us in Christ. If one person comes to it through the baptism of the Spirit, or another one through the experience of holiness, or another one through a deep experience of the cross, or another one through an experience of something else, I thank God if all of us come into the good of what is ours in Christ.

I used to be very much against the baptism of the Spirit because I had been taught from the beginning that the baptism of the Spirit was ours at birth. The Holy Spirit came into us at birth, and I believe it. He does come into us at birth, and the empowering from on high is ours at birth, but how many Christians may I ask, enter into it at birth? It was theirs but they did not enter into it. There is a lot of excess attached to it sometimes. (I know perhaps of one or two in my whole experience who have entered into it at birth.) Nevertheless, I have to confess this: Many people who have had a very real second experience of the Holy Spirit have had their lives transformed. Because of our theological conceptions, we are not going to turn a blind eye to that. Thank God for it! Everyone who can be changed, let's have them all changed. We want them to be changed the right way. We want them to get into the good of it in the best way. If it has to come sometimes through some odd ways; let it, so long as we are in the good of all that is ours in Christ.

I heard of a Scots lady who had a Sunday school class a little while ago, and I think some of the children were very near to a very terrible fact. She had taught her Sunday school class the chorus: "I will make you fishers of men." And to her horror when they stood up to sing, she heard that they had got it quite wrong. Of course, she had sung it to them correctly, but they all sang: "I will make you vicious old men. I will make you vicious old men." I am afraid there are many Christians of whom it must be said that they have become vicious old men and women. I know it sounds terrible to say it, but some parts of the mission field are wrecked and ruined by vicious people. And so is the church by people who have it all in their head—they know Spurgeon, they know Murray, they know this, they know that, they take the Westminster Record and many other things, and yet there is not one bit of difference in their lives. I could give you so many illustrations.

When I was a lad and first saved, I was brought up on victory teaching, and I'm afraid that because I was brought up on victory teaching, I had a thing in the end against it. Everyone was victorious, and everyone who ever entered the pulpit used to tell us about the victory life. I used to sit in the congregation and think to myself that I was of all men the most miserable, for I was the only one in the vast congregation who was not living the victory life. They all smiled so sweetly when they sang those hymns about victory living and so on. Then I found out, in talking with many, that one after another had no experience of victory at all. But the greatest shock I ever got was some years later. When speaking to a dear friend, I learned that he had once challenged the brother I had heard speak that day. My friend had asked him, "Do you really know this victory?" "Oh no," he said, "Brother, I preach it by faith." So we were all living in a deception. Victory had been preached to us and we all thought that everyone had got it, and none of us had got it at all.

I remember once, dear Mr. Redpath had a youngish man go up to him after one of the big meetings, one of the big campaigns in Richmond when I was first saved. He said quite loudly in front of quite a few people who were in the inquiry meeting: "Brother, I was saved two years ago. Hallelujah! One and a half years ago, I received the baptism of the Holy Spirit, and a half year ago I was made perfect." (I know this from Mr. Redpath because he often used it as an illustration.) Mr. Redpath looked at him and said, "My dear young man, I am very glad to meet you indeed, for you have gotten somewhere the apostle Paul never got in a whole lifetime." I have never forgotten—he was perfectly sinless. Someone went up to Moody and told him that he was perfectly sinless, and Moody said, "I would like to have a talk with your wife."

You get this kind of thing again and again. There are people who deceive themselves into believing that they have an experience. We have to be careful. There are things and experiences which are erroneous. There are things which are counterfeit. To say the least, there are things which are a pretense, so we have to be careful. But if we are abiding in Christ, and we are discerning what is coming and yet are open all the time to what is ours, we can take it by faith. We should be going on into an ever-increasing experience of all that is ours in Him. The need is not head knowledge but revelation so that faith can appropriate. Head knowledge puts it in our head, but we do not have it in our heart. However, when the eyes of our heart see, faith leaps out and appropriates what is ours.

I hope this has been of some value to you. I hope that you will go away and ask the Lord: "Lord, are there areas in my great salvation that was given to me in which somehow I am failing to appropriate?" Even if we have an experience of all four, we have to come back again and again to discover there is more of Christ in every one. I am coming back to find there is more in justification than I ever thought when I was first saved. I never realised it then. Now I understand it more and more, and I receive Christ. I think it is a more and more wonderful thing to understand what God has done in us. How anyone can preach the gospel, it's a weakness with me, until a person sees the wonder of being justified, I don't know. It is a most marvellous thing if a few of us can see it, so we need our eyes opened.

I was saved in 1943, but it was in January, 1949 that for the first time I had the experience of the Spirit and the cross—the indwelling of the Spirit and the cross, of being crucified with Christ. It had been mine in 1943 when I came to Christ, yet all those years from 1943–1949, six years, I lived in the wilderness, desperately trying to live the Christian life and failing terribly. Then one day I read a little book entitled, But How? Because so often I said to myself: but how? I listened to Mr. Redpath and others, Keswick speakers in Richmond, and I used to say, "But how?" We used to sing, "my chains fell off," and I used to think: but how? And when this little book was sent to me by the pastor, But How? I realised someone else had asked that question. I spent a whole afternoon on my knees reading that tiny, little book, six or seven pages, perhaps fifteen. It was just as if an angel read it to me. Heaven opened and the eyes of my heart saw for the first time. I knew that I had never felt such an incredible fool. When I saw that the Holy Spirit was within me, I thought to myself, "What a fool I have been! He is in me to live the Christian life and I just simply ignored Him and tried to live it without Him. Thank God, from that day to this, with all my own faults and failings, I have never ever tried to live the Christian life since then to this day. I can say that truthfully. I have just left it to the Lord and trusted Him moment by moment. And I believe I have something more to learn from this as well. The great thing is we need the eyes of our heart enlightened. Don't get disillusioned by thinking, "Oh, it does not work for me. I cannot understand it." What is wrong with you is that you have it up in your head, but you do not have it down in your heart. So go away and say, "Lord, enlighten the eyes of my heart. I need to see it; I need to get into the good of it so I can see what is mine and start to appropriate it." May the Lord help us.

Lord, Jesus, we do ask Thee that Thou wouldst use this evening to bring a number of us to a knowledge of our need. Thou hast made such a great provision for us in our Lord Jesus. Our salvation is so great. Now Lord, we pray together that Thou wouldst open the eyes of our hearts to see what we need. One of us may need to know Thine indwelling; another one to know what it is to be crucified and buried and risen; another one needs to know more about being justified. All of us surely need to know more about the anointing, the empowering of Thy Spirit. Lord, we bring this all to Thee, and we ask Thee that Thou wouldst help us to be spiritually intelligent in our seeking of Thee, so that we may be able to see where we have areas of need and we can say, 'Lord, open our eyes to see what is ours.' Lord, You have done it all. Calvary is a fact, Pentecost is a fact, the work of the cross is finished, and the Holy Spirit has been given. Oh, Father, we pray that Thou wouldst bring every one of us into the full good of what Thou hast done through Calvary and Pentecost. We ask it in Thy name. Amen.

4.
The Trial of Faith

I Peter 1:1–7

Peter, an apostle of Jesus Christ, to the elect who are sojourners of the Dispersion in Pontus, Galatia, Cappadocia, Asia and Bithynia, according to the foreknowledge of God the Father, in sanctification of the Spirit, unto obedience and sprinkling of the blood of Jesus Christ: Grace to you and peace be multiplied. Blessed be the God and Father of our Lord Jesus Christ, who according to his great mercy begat us again unto a living hope by the resurrection of Jesus Christ from the dead, unto an inheritance incorruptible, and undefiled, and that fadeth not away, reserved in heaven for you, who by the power of God are guarded, through faith unto a salvation ready to be revealed in the last time. Wherein ye greatly rejoice, though now for a little while, if need be, ye have been put to grief in manifold trials, that the proof of your faith, being more precious than gold that perisheth though it is proved by fire, may be found   *unto praise and glory and honor at the revelation of Jesus Christ.*

The Great Mercy of God

The phrase I want to take out is in verse 7, translated in the Standard Version and in the Revised Version as "the proof of your faith," and in the Authorised Version "the trial of your faith." First of all, note to whom this is being addressed. Who are these who are knowing the trial of their faith? They are those who through the great mercy of God have been begotten again unto a living hope by the resurrection of Jesus Christ from the dead. It is every man or woman who has proved in their experience that Jesus Christ is alive from the dead and is able to say. That is the folk that Peter is speaking to. I want you to notice that it begins with the great mercy of God, and I think that the more we go on with the Lord, the more we discover how great the mercy of God is. I must say that for myself, and I suppose for many others that when we first came to the Lord, we talked about the mercy of the Lord, but it did not really mean such a lot to us. Of course, we knew our sins were forgiven, and we knew the Lord had shown love to us. Nevertheless, it seems to me that as we go on with the Lord we discover how really great the mercy of the Lord is. Not only did He save us at the beginning but that He has ever continued with us.

Again, I want you to notice that it was through this great mercy that God saved you. Remember, God knows everything about you long before you were saved. He knew everything about you before you were born. God knows everything about you, so it really was great mercy. It is not as if God saved you and as time has gone on He has discovered all kinds of things about you which could give Him second thoughts. It was great mercy that He saved you because He knew the worst about you. He knew the potential for evil in your life; He knew the potential for duplicity in your life. He knew all this when He saved you. It was through His great mercy He begot us again, that He brought us to a spiritual birth to a living hope by the resurrection of Jesus Christ from the dead. We are born again because Jesus is alive. Legally we could be saved by the death of Jesus Christ. His blood would still cancel out our sin, but then we would be left in the unenviable position of having our sins forgiven, cleansed away, without a knowledge of the life and power of God within us. It is because Jesus Christ is risen from the dead, He is alive from the dead that we are born of God's Spirit. For it says in John 1:12–13: "As many as received him," (that is the One risen from the dead) "to them gave he the right to become children of God, even to them that believe on his name: who were born, not of blood, nor of the will of the flesh, nor of the will of man, but of God."

A Living Hope

What is this living hope? It is a living hope, It is a vital hope. It is a hope that is not just a dead hope, an abstract hope, but a hope that is alive—alive in us. What is this living hope? Isn't it Christ in you the hope of glory? That is the living hope. We have not just been saved from our sin; we have not even just been born of the Spirit of God. We have been given this living hope of Christ in us, the hope of glory. As someone said in one of the renderings, "Because we are part of Christ." God in His great grace has made us part of Christ and Christ part of us. There is a union that has taken place. Christ in you the hope of glory.

What is glory? How marvellous it is that one day, whoever we are, however insignificant we are, however weak we are, however small we are, however unworthy we have been in the past, whatever there is of Christ, that is going to be glorified. So if there is a lot of Christ, there will be a lot of glory, and if there is little of Christ in my life there will be little of glory. Whatever there is of Christ in me is going to be glorified because He is the certain hope of glory. No matter who you are or what you are, if you have received Christ, if there is something of Christ's life and nature in you, that is going to be glorified.

An Inheritance

This living hope brings us to an inheritance incorruptible and undefiled and that fadeth not away. What is this inheritance? Our so great salvation introduces us into this inheritance; but what is the inheritance? Surely this inheritance again is this living hope. It is Christ the Bridegroom. We are going to come to Him; we are going to be joined to Him. One day the marriage supper of the Lamb is going to take place. We can say the Lord is my portion. That is my inheritance—incorruptible, undefiled, and that fadeth not away. It is not a thing; it is a Person. Of course, there will be a lot of things also because we are heirs of God and joint heirs with Him, but how marvellous it is that as His bride we are going to enter into all that God has laid up for His Son.

Everything God has conceived and thought of for His Son, all that He is going to do through His Son, all that He has planned for His Son, you and I as part of the bride are going to enter into that. It is an inheritance, incorruptible, undefiled, that fadeth not away.

I always get a picture of someone dying and leaving certain things in the loft or the attic. Maybe there are beautiful drapes or curtains, but they fade. There are other things that get defiled and get dirty when they are stored, or other things that corrupt. But here is an inheritance that cannot corrupt, an inheritance that cannot be defiled, an inheritance that does not fade. No! Not when we have been with Him for a million, million, million years will one little bit of the glory have faded.

We human beings get so familiar with things, don't we? We get so utterly familiar. We say familiarity breeds contempt, but there will be nothing like that with God. It will never fade. The Lord has said of our way down here that the path of the just is as a shining light. It shineth more and more unto the perfect day or to noonday (see Proverbs 4:18). Surely if it is going to be, or should be, like that down here, it ought to be in eternity like that so that it will be more glory and more glory and more glory and more glory.

A Glorious Future with the Lord

We do not know what God has got in store for us. We just have no idea what God has got in store. We are somehow imprisoned in our concept—by all that we know, by time, by all that is transient, and by the things around us. It is only natural; we are finite and therefore this is all we have ever known. Everything we know really has a beginning and an end. We cannot conceive what is in the mind of God for eternity. We cannot conceive what it was in the mind of God to do from the start in mankind. All we know is that when this sinful era of human history, with all its glorious revelation of the grace of God and the love of God, the mercy of God, the lovingkindness of God, when that is over and done with God is going to go on with the real job. And no one really knows what the real job is, except that God is going to go on with that real job.

As we have often said to you, a marriage is either an end or a beginning, whichever way you care to look at it. The Bible ends with a marriage, and surely the whole point of it is that it is an end of one phase and the beginning of another. It is an end of one whole era in which God revealed His glorious grace to sinful and fallen man and an opening of a new era where there is no more sin, no more death, no more corruption, no more mourning, and no more crying. We cannot conceive of such a time. Some people have actually dared to say that it will be boring. Now I know that causes some evangelicals to get terribly upset, but I have great sympathy with people who think like that because naturally that is how we ought to think. How utterly boring! There will be no ups and downs, no crises, no dangers. Just imagine a life where everything is perfect, everything is right—all very well for a holiday.

Think about it. You may think that you long for that time, but after a few years of it you might think: "Oh!" just like we used to in Egypt with those brazen blue skies day after day. In the second year it rained for ten minutes and the boys went wild. They ran out and stood in a few little drops of water, and again and again I heard them say to one another, "I would give anything to have a foggy day." The most popular picture we had was in my office, which was a picture of Richmond Park in the fog. It was a rather lovely picture, I must say, because it had some deer looming out of the mist. The boys used to come and look at that because it reminded them of England. Yet, now that we are back here, we long for those brazen skies, the sunshine, and the settled climate.

I have sympathy with people who think like that. It is because we cannot somehow adjust ourselves to exactly what God is going to do, and it comes from a misconception of God. God cannot be boring! If I may put it rather crudely and tritely, God is the most exciting Person in the universe. He is always doing something. He always has plans afoot. The fact is we have a glorious future, a glorious future and it is summed up in the word "glory". That's it! It is summed up in this word. Don't think, you dear little Christian, that all you are is someone who is just sort of at the mercy of Satan now and again in an unbelieving world, and you have to go through it all with a few tears and a few sorrows, sing a few hymns, say a few prayers, come along to this meeting, if you can bear it, and put up with the saints here. Then, one day you are going to go to heaven and that's that. Then, you will sit around doing nothing for all eternity. Never! There is a most tremendous future. We have no idea!

If this world is so beautiful, so glorious in its design, in its fallen condition, whatever was in the mind of God originally? When it is all over, what do we have? We have a marriage supper, a marvellous marriage supper. So glorious is the prospect, so enthralling is the future that the Lord says, "Blessed are those that are even invited to the marriage supper of the Lamb, just to get a look in on this, let alone be the bride. Oh, it is going to be such a blessing because there is a tremendous future ahead that we have absolutely no idea of. Do you honestly think that God is less clever and less ingenious than the American space program? If man in his fallen state can do these amazing things that are making the whole world marvel, how much more will God one day be doing things that will make us all marvel, and they will really be marvellous.

Kept by the Power of God

Well, we must not stop there. This is unto a living hope, to an inheritance incorruptible. And hear this; this is the thing we all need. "Who by the power of God are guarded." Don't we need to know it? How few Christians know anything about the pattern prayer which the Lord Jesus taught us to pray! "Lead us not into temptation, but deliver us from the evil one." There is far too much of this crass idea that you can just somehow or other walk into temptation and God will keep you. Jesus taught us to pray: "Deliver us from temptation. Lead us not into temptation but deliver us from the evil one." It is the fear of the Lord which is the beginning of wisdom.

By the power of God we are kept or guarded unto this salvation which is ready to be revealed. You are already saved, so how come you have a salvation ready to be revealed? That's it. One day, and maybe all of us shall see it with these eyes. One day, the trumpet of God is going to sound and the Lord is going to come, and the salvation, which Peter talks about here, will be revealed.

It is ready to be revealed at the last time. Aren't we in the last time waiting for that revelation of the salvation into which we have been brought by the grace of God, the final consummation of the salvation which by His grace and great mercy has brought us to?

"Kept by the power of God." Do we know anything about the ability of God to keep someone? It is all there. If you and I want to know something about the inheritance, if we want to be prepared and trained for the inheritance, if we would be those who have much of Christ that He might increase as we decrease, we have to know the power of God keeping us. God has to chisel such a lot away. God has to break us in so many unbreakable places. God has to shape us in a way that we do not want to be shaped. If only it could all be left to ourselves so that we could be spontaneous and free and happy. But if we want that living hope, if the self has got to decrease, my word that is a painful business! If God starts to bring us into conditions and circumstances through which He will break the unbreakable, through which He will shape the unshapeable, and through which He will really do this work, we have got to know the power of God. Only the power of God will keep us when God Himself has led us into trial. Don't you see that? We need to be kept by the power of God when we are in this situation. God does not want to save us from lions. He wants to put us amongst the lions, and then we find they cannot bite us. That is God's way. He does not want to save us from the furnace of fire. He wants us to go into it and find the One who is like unto the Son of God in the midst of the fire. That is the way that we are to know what it is to be guarded or kept by the power of God.

That brings me to the next phrase. All that is the explanation for these trials of your faith. In the Authorised Version we have the word "trial," and in the Revised Version we have the word "proof." In a way it is very hard, I think, to really give this word its proper meaning because if you say "proof," I think you lose something of the sense of testing and trying. If you say "trial," you lose something of the feeling of proof, for the word means that God only tries what is there. In other words, God never allows a person to come into temptation above that they are able. Of this you can be absolutely certain if you are in a situation, which you find very difficult, unless it is through your own foolishness. I have to say this, that through our own foolishness we can uncover ourselves. This is what it means when we say, "Lead us not into temptation." We can make big claims like Peter when he said: "I will die with You." Satan went into the presence of the Lord and said, "Can I have him?" And God said, "Yes." The Lord Jesus said to Peter: "I prayed for you that your faith will not fail." We can make big claims sometimes, which are heard, and then we can uncover ourselves.

Greatly Rejoice

Nevertheless, if we have committed to God and if we want the Lord to do this work, there will be these times of trial. Now here is a great comfort to us. God never tries what is not there. We can get the idea from this trial of our faith that God is sort of limited, and He is just trying to break up everything. He is trying to get rid of everything, but that is not the point at all. The point is that there is something so precious, much more precious than gold which perishes (if you can think of such a thing), something so precious that God says, "I am going to try this to prove it." In other words, the trial of your faith is to prove that the faith is there, not to prove that it is not there. So rejoice. That is why James says, "Rejoice, count it all joy, my brethren, when you fall into manifold trials" (see 1:2). What on earth does he mean? He means, look at it this way: there is something very precious there that God is allowing to be tried. Of course, it is all very well for us to stand up here talking like this, but when we are in it, it is quite different, isn't it? Nevertheless, the trial of your faith is so important.

Have you ever noticed how in the temple and in the different visions of the city, in Ezekiel and Revelation, there is a man measuring everything? All the time everything is being measured. Why do we need an angelic person or someone like the Son of Man measuring everything which God is revealing anyway and giving us the measurements? God is actually giving us the measurements. Some people avoid Ezekiel because it is so filled with measurements. This should be so many cubits, that should be so many cubits, every little thing, even washbowls are mentioned and everything is according to measurements. Then you have this man going around measuring, measuring, measuring. He even measures the river. In the book of Revelation you have the man going around with a golden measuring rod measuring everything, yet you are told the measurements. So why does he measure? It is a marvellous picture of this trial of your faith. God is very, very careful that nothing goes through but the pure life and nature of Jesus Christ in us. So it is all being measured. Every bit.

To Praise, to Glory, and to Honor

So why are we to know the trial of our faith? That it "may be found unto praise and glory and honor at the revelation of Jesus Christ" (1 Peter 7b). There it is. So do not look upon the negative side of it. Every time you are in a trial of your faith it is that it may be to praise, to glory and to honor. What does that mean? First of all, it is to His praise. One day in heaven, one day in the kingdom, people will know your story and they will praise the Lord. They will say, "Did you see the amazing way the Lord took old So-and-So through life? Isn't that amazing? Did you hear about it!? The Lord just put the pressure right on, then brought in this, and brought in that, and the faith that came out!" It will be to praise! What a story it will be!

We all love the stories in the Old Testament, and the stories in the book of Acts. That is nothing, as dear old Broadbent once said, to the story, which has been written ever since up there. The whole thing is being recorded. It says so: "The Lord hearkened and wrote a book of remembrance" (Malachi 3:16). One day when the pages are opened, the whole thing will be there, the inner story. We will not be saying, "Hudson Taylor, oh marvellous man!" We shall be saying, "What a marvellous Lord!" C. T. Studd, mind you, he has been done a lot of harm by some of the things said about him, but still when we are up there, we will say, "My, my, what a Lord! Praise, glory, and honor!

What is honor? Honor means that you are going to be put into a position and you will be honored because of it. In other words, you will be given a place in the administration of heaven and the government of heaven. You will be honored; not empty honors, but honors that mean something because they are based in spiritual history and experience. Can't we thank the Lord for all of that?

Examples of the Trial of Faith

All the way through the Bible we find this principle: the trial of your faith. Take Joseph. God tried everything in Joseph's life. It says in Psalm 105:19: "Until the time that his word came to pass, the word of the Lord tried him." But that can be true of every one of them.

God said to Abraham to get out into a land that He would show him. Then what did God do? He never actually gave Abraham that land in the whole of his life. He even had to buy the burial plot, which is there today, for his wife Sarah and for the family. God never gave it to him. If the Word of the Lord was tried, it was the trial of his faith. God said, "In your seed shall all the nations of the earth be blessed." Yet God waited and waited and waited until Abraham was one hundred years of age and Sarah was ninety. Can you imagine it?! When they were sixty or seventy they must have had a little talk about it and said, "it is going to be a miracle," but when they were a hundred—it is incredible! Yet that is what it says about them.

Romans 4:17–20: "(As it is written, A father of many nations have I made thee) before him whom he believed, even God, who giveth life to the dead, and calleth the things that are not, as though they were. Who in hope believed against hope, to the end that he might become a father of many nations, according to that which had been spoken, so shall thy seed be. And without being weakened in faith he considered his own body now as good as dead (he being about a hundred years old), and the deadness of Sarah's womb; yet, looking unto the promise of God, he wavered not through unbelief, but waxed strong through faith."

There are only two things that can happen when we are in the trial of our faith. One is that we collapse into unbelief; the other is that we wax strong in faith. Every time there is a trial of our faith, our faith comes through like gold refined in the fire. It is deeper, fuller, purer, and stronger.

It does not matter where you turn. Look at the way the Lord dealt with Moses. Forty years in the desert is enough to destroy any real hope that something would happen. You do not generally think of a man entering into his real ministry when he is eighty years of age, but he started at eighty years of age. Even he thought it was over. He said to God: "Just remember that I cannot talk. I am a stammerer." And the Lord said to him, "All right, you take Aaron." From then on Moses did all the talking and Aaron did all the acting. It was a most extraordinary thing. God humored him. So deeply had Moses been dealt with by God in those forty years—the Word of the Lord tried him.

David is another picture of it. How the Word of the Lord tried David! He knew he was to be king. Remember when Samuel anointed him and said that he would be king? He knew it, yet all through those years the Word of the Lord tried him.

I think of the apostle Paul when he said in II Corinthians 12:2–4: "I was caught up into the third heaven and heard things that was not lawful for a man even to utter." And then he said, "There was given to me a messenger of Satan a thorn in the flesh" (v.7). Here was the trial of his faith. It got him down—the great apostle Paul. It got him down so much he sought the Lord and all he got was, "My grace is sufficient for thee" (v. 9). In other words, "My grace is enough for this." Three times it happened, at the time this letter was written. We do not know if after that many more occasions came. However, we know at least three occasions when the apostle Paul went to the Lord and sought Him about this terrible thing, whatever it was. It was the trial of his faith.

See What God Has Done!

I think we should always be thankful to God when we have any experience of being tried because it is a sign that there is something there to be tried. God never puts anyone into the fire in which He knows there is nothing but chaff. He will only allow to go through what there is really of Himself. God would have refused Satan's request to have Peter if He had known that there was not a little atom of faith that could come through. That is a very sobering thought, a very sobering thought, because it means sometimes when we look at some people and see what is happening in their lives. We cannot understand: How did he come through? I am sure I wouldn't have. The fact is you are quite right; that is why God does not put you through it. God will only permit those to go through that where He knows there is something. One day those will be the very people who vindicate the Lord when we are in the kingdom and before His face. It will be with praise and worship as we look back upon the whole of our lives and see what God has done in them. It will be with praise. We shall vindicate the Lord. He will not vindicate Himself.

We will vindicate Him and say, "Right and just were all Thy judgments and all Thy ways."

Shall we pray?

Beloved Lord, we do pray together that we may know what it is to really walk with Thee and to know that power of Thine which is able to keep us to that salvation which in the end is going to be revealed. Lord, Thou knowest in every one of our lives what there is of Thyself, and Thou knowest how much Thou canst prove it. We do praise Thee every time we go through an experience in which we come out with a proof of divine faith. Father, we do pray that Thou wilt help every one of us. If there are any who are in the midst of a trial of their faith—something in the home, something in the office, something in their personal lives, something here in the church, in the company, something Lord, that Thou hast said is being tried—we pray beloved Lord, that Thou wilt watch over them that their faith fail not and bring them through with the proof of their faith. And so, dear Lord, we commit ourselves now to Thee in the name of our Lord Jesus Christ. Amen.

5.
Appropriating What is Ours in Christ

We have speaking about some of the characteristics that God looks for in those who would really serve Him. We have spoken of utter devotion to Christ, leading to worship, service, and testimony. We have spoken of an implicit faith in God and in His Word. We have spoken of a clear understanding of God's purpose and objective, and of an ever-increasing experience of all that God has provided for us in and through Christ. If we are going to serve the Lord, we cannot afford to become static. We have got to have an ever-increasing experience of the Lord, not just merely an ever-increasing knowledge of the Lord, but an ever-increasing experience of the Lord.

First of all, we have spoken of the point that God has made everything ours. He has made all provision for us in Christ. Everything we need for our personal life or for our corporate life has been provided by God in Christ. There is nothing necessary, essential to the Christian life or to the church, which God has not provided in Christ. It is all there.

Then we spoke about the secret of abiding in Him, remaining where God has placed us in Christ. The root cause of nearly all Christian breakdown, corporate or personal, is that people do not abide in Christ. They do not learn to distinguish those things that draw them out of Christ, as it were, entice them out of Christ. They often go out to meet the enemy or they go off to some thing as a thing, an experience as an experience, without realising it. It all seems so good. The devil comes as an angel of light. It seems so wonderful, so good, but then we are found outside of Christ. The enemy's whole objective is to divorce us practically and experientially from Christ. Abiding in Him is the secret, and the Lord Jesus said a lot about abiding in Him and He in us.

We also spoke about the fact that if everything is provided for us in Christ, and we have been placed in Christ, and all we have to do is remain or continue where God has placed us, then why are we often so defeated? Why are we often living in a superficial way? Why are we so poverty stricken spiritually, so powerless? Why is there so much that is weak in a wrong way about us as God's children and so much else? Why is there so much contradiction? The simple point of the matter is that we need to appropriate what is ours in Christ. God has provided it all but it is to be appropriated by faith. In other words, until you see it, and you believe it, and you take it, it is not yours. That was so of salvation. Until you saw that Christ had died for you and you were a sinner and needed to be saved, until you believed that He had died to save you and was able to save you, and until you took your salvation by faith and cast yourself upon Christ, you were not saved. It is the same with every other step in the Christian life. It has to be appropriated by faith, and this again is the little key into everything. For we can be in Christ, Christ can be in us, we can be abiding in Christ, we can learn to abide in Christ, and still we are impoverished and we cannot understand why. It is perhaps because our eyes are not open to all that is ours, so we just wonder. We are not appropriating. Of course, you can understand that the devil has a vested interest in spiritual eye diseases. I think the biggest need amongst God's children is for the healing and cure of eye disease, for everything in the end goes back to it.

The Four-fold Way of God's Provision

We spoke last time of the fact that all that God has provided in Christ is given to us in a four-fold way through Calvary and Pentecost. Christ is our full salvation, and we have divided it into two—salvation through Christ, who has been given to us first through Calvary and then through Pentecost. It is first through the cross and then by the Spirit. There are two sides to the work of Calvary: first we are justified and secondly we are crucified. And there are two sides to the work of Pentecost: first we are indwelt and secondly we are empowered. It is interesting that being justified and being indwelt are often linked together, and being crucified and being empowered are brought together. These two complement each other; one side of the cross is complemented by one side of Pentecost, and the other side of the cross is complemented by the other side of Pentecost.

I ended by saying something about never letting theology stop you from seeking more of Christ. There is a great mistake when theology gets in our way, when we just simply have some conception. It may be a right conception, but because of a kind of clinical approach to spiritual things we are stopped from seeking the Lord for something more. Even with the most correct knowledge, there is sometimes in experience a very real lacks. God has to be sovereign in the way that He brings us into all that is ours in Christ.

The Need for Revelation

As I said, the need is not head knowledge, but it is revelation so that faith can appropriate. For it is when the eyes of our hearts are enlightened that faith spontaneously springs into action. You cannot force yourself to take a faith position. If you have not seen, no amount of coercion will get you into it. All you will do is try desperately to take some position which will not work, and in the end you will say it does not work. No, it does not work with you because you have not seen. The whole question of revelation is vital, and this is where, in fact, we have to be very humble indeed. For you see we may have great brains, or we may have a lot of knowledge, or great wills, or great feelings, or zeal for the Lord, or devotion for the Lord, but in the end we all have to come to our knees like little children and ask the Lord to open our eyes. This is the safety of it all, the security. We all have to come like little children from the greatest to the smallest and ask the Lord: "Lord, enlighten the eyes of my heart. Give me a spirit of wisdom and revelation and enlighten the eyes of my heart that I may know, that I might see."

Brother Nee has pointed out that before we can reckon ourselves dead indeed unto sin, we must first know that our old man has been crucified with Christ. And this is so important, for it is not knowing in our head but knowing in our heart. It is the heart's apprehension of what God has done at Calvary so that the eyes of our hearts see, suddenly see, and we are in the good of it.

I can only give you my own little experience in this matter. I was brought up in a very keen company. I was saved in 1943, but it was in 1949 that for the first time I came into an experience of the cross and the Holy Spirit. I have looked back upon it many, many times. I must have heard the indwelling of Christ in the Spirit emphasised again and again, but in spite of the fact that I must have sung about it, read about it in the Word, heard it preached, gone to Bible studies on it, it never dawned on me. It was not until that day in January 1949 that it just broke upon me, and the eyes of my heart saw it. When I saw it, it was just as if I had never seen it before, as if I had never heard it. Frankly, I really did look upon the company of Christians I was in almost as spiritual ignoramuses. I could not think how on earth I had never heard it, but in fact it was me. They might have been shouting it from the rooftops to me, but I had not seen it, so it did not mean anything to me. But I want to make that very clear. Once we have seen something, we go out to it in faith. Spontaneously, faith goes out and appropriates what is ours. This is of the utmost importance, and it is why Paul is always praying that we might see and know.

We want to look at these four points more closely, remembering that they in fact do overlap. These four points are justified, crucified, indwelt, empowered. We want to look at them a little more clearly. Of course, they overlap each other. You cannot be clinical about these things, and you cannot actually wholly define them. It is interesting that in Galatians 2:20 Paul brought two of them together. He said, "I have been crucified with Christ, nevertheless I live, yet not I but Christ liveth in me (indwelling)." And then he says, "And I live by the faith of the Son of God who loved me and gave himself for me." That is justification. So in fact, he brings all three together in one point. But sometimes it helps us to analyse and define these things a little more. It may be that we shall discover there is an area of need, which God has provided for us in Christ, and it may help us to go back and really start to seek the Lord that He will open our eyes to this matter.

Justified—Christ for Us

The first matter is to be justified and I have very simply described this as "Christ for us." The word justified literally means "to declare right." That means you are declared right or you are made right or the other word is to acquit. You are acquitted. Let's look at a number of Scriptures.

> "Yet knowing that a man is not justified by the
> works of the law but through faith in Jesus Christ,
> even we believed on Christ Jesus, that we might be
> justified by faith in Christ." Galatians 2:16

> "So that the law is become our tutor to bring us unto Christ,
> that we might be justified by faith." Galatians 3:24

*"Being therefore justified by faith, we have peace
with God through our Lord Jesus Christ; through
whom also we have had our access by faith into
this grace wherein we stand." Romans 5:1–2*

It is interesting to note in those two verses three things. We have peace, we have access, and we stand. Those are three things connected with justification. We have peace, we have access, and we stand, we have standing.

*"Who shall lay anything to the charge of God's elect? It
is God that justifieth; who is he that condemneth? It
is Christ Jesus that died, yea rather, that was raised
from the dead, who is at the right hand of God, who
also maketh intercession for us." Romans 8:33*

These three things are connected to our justification—Christ died, Christ was raised and Christ intercedes for us. These are the three great points to do with our justification. This is absolutely fundamental. You have to have some knowledge of this; otherwise you cannot be a child of God. Although every single one of us who is a child of God has had experience of justification, it is amazing how weak an appreciation we can get through on. It seems as though the Lord falls over Himself to save us, and if we have the weakest appreciation, the slightest glimmer of understanding, He saves us.

One of the weaknesses of many Christians is that we are not absolutely clear as to our justification. What has God done? I think it comes out in a lot of our preaching. We can ask people to come to Christ, but very few people can preach the gospel because they have very little real appreciation of what it means to be justified. In my own ministry, I find it to be a peculiarly difficult thing to preach about the grace of God and the justification of God. Yet I see more and more that this is not just a spiritual kindergarten matter. It is absolutely fundamental to every part of our spiritual well being. There are many Christians who know a lot about the cross, but because they do not know enough about justification, they are tormented by feelings of unworthiness, feelings of darkness, and feelings of uncleanness. When the Lord begins to work and remove what we are, when He really starts to get to grips with our self-life, woe betide us if we do not have a strong appreciation and understanding of our justification. I think all of us need it. It needs to be understood much more than it is and it needs to be appropriated.

Oh, if everyone were to appropriate something more of what God has provided for us in our justification, it would be a tremendous thing. The Sunday morning time around the Lord's Table would be filled with praise. There would be people who have not opened their lips for years who would be bubbling out in praise, real praise, and some possibly who would be held back just a little. But certainly there would be a lot of people who are not praising the Lord who would suddenly find themselves overwhelmed by the love and the grace of God. It is a tremendous thing!

Pardon

These are the main points of our justification. We are pardoned. 1 John 1:9: "If we confess our sins, He is faithful and just to forgive us our sins, and to cleanse us from all unrighteousness." How beautiful that is! It is not, if we confessed our sins, but if we confess our sins, He is faithful. It is not He was faithful, but He is faithful and just. It is not faithful and loving, but faithful and just. In other words, this question of justification is absolutely legal. It is not that God is trying to get round something because He loves us. He has legally cleared away our sins, and when God Himself legitimately, legally clears away our sin, who can bring it up? The great Law-giver Himself, has found a way of canceling out all our sin and blotting it out of the record altogether. Then who can bring it up? What an amazing thing it is to be a child of God! Pardoned—what a wonderful thing!

1 John 2:12 says, "I write unto you, my little children, because your sins are forgiven you for his name's sake." What a lovely word forgiveness is. God has forgiven us. That is very, very wonderful. And I often think that it is only when you and I begin to understand what our sin is that we appreciate what God's forgiveness is. "She who has been forgiven much will also love much" (see Luke 7:47). This is a great law. In Ephesians 1:7 we are told we have the forgiveness of all our trespasses.

"Blessed is he whose transgression is forgiven: whose sin is covered...I acknowledged my sin, unto thee, and mine iniquity did I not hide: I said, I will confess my transgressions

unto the Lord: and thou forgavest the iniquity of my sin."
Oh, what a beautiful word—pardon. Psalm 32:1, 5

Cleansing

Then there is cleansing. 1 John 1:7: "But if we walk in the light, as he is in the light, we have fellowship one with another, and the blood of Jesus his Son cleanseth us from all sin." There is cleansing for all sin if we walk in the light. In other words, do not hold it back. Don't try to bury it, but come out into the light and there is cleansing.

"Come now, and let us reason together, saith the Lord: though your sins be as scarlet, they shall be as white as snow" (see Isaiah 1:18). What a wonderful thing it is to have sins like scarlet made white as snow! It is remarkable! Cleansing. Only the blood of Christ can cleanse scarlet into white.

In that beautiful verse in Revelation 1:5 we have this other rendering in the RV, which I think, is correct: "Unto him that loveth us, and loosed us from our sins." The AV has "washed us from our sins," but loosed us is much stronger. The word means to dissolve. Who has dissolved our sins or freed us from our sins or even destroyed our sins. What a wonderful word! He has freed us from our sins. They are gone, absolutely gone; you will never see them again. Some of us rake them up. They are like antiques. We keep them all beautifully polished and draped around the room so we can look at them. Or we take them to other people and show them to them and now and again we have a bad time about their state and condition. But God has gotten rid of the lot, and He will never make mention of them. Some Christians talk so much about their sins, but one day in glory it is a word that is taboo as far as God is concerned. They are blotted out. There is no record of them. It is almost as if you say, "Sin," and God would say to you, "Sin? Never heard of it in connection with you. It is gone. Whatever are you talking about?"

God only knows of righteousness, the righteousness of His Son. Christ became our sin. If you say, the sins of Christ, God will say, "I know all those. I know all about that." But if you say anything about your sins, God says, "I don't know anything about that. I have no record of it, no record at all. Go to the books, to the archives, to the registry office. You will not find anything there. It is all cancelled out, blotted out, cleansed." Well, I think that is simply wonderful.

"If any man sin, we have an Advocate with the Father, Jesus Christ the righteous" (1 John 2:1). Do you know that the word Advocate is Comforter? He is one who comes alongside. Of course, this is no ground for carrying on in sin, but it is wonderful to know that there is cleansing from sin.

Covering

"Even the righteousness of God through faith in Jesus Christ unto all and upon them all that believe" (Romans 3:22). Isn't that wonderful? The righteousness of God unto all and upon all that believe. Covering. It is given to us; it is upon us, the righteousness of Christ.

"Him who knew no sin God made to be sin on our behalf; that we might become the righteousness of God in him" (II Corinthians 5:21). You and I have become the righteousness of God in Christ.

We have been placed in Christ and we have been covered in His righteousness. We have become the righteousness of God in Him—covering.

We are not only covered, we are absolutely clothed in the righteousness of Christ. If you abide in Him and walk in the light the garments will not be soiled, for they are the robes, the garment of His righteousness.

Reconciliation

Reconciliation is another thing to do with justification. "God was in Christ reconciling the world unto himself, not reckoning unto them their trespasses" (II Corinthians 5:19). God was reconciling. This word means being brought back into oneness, brought back to God—reconciled.

"And you, being in time past alienated and enemies in your mind in your evil works, yet now hath he reconciled in the body of his flesh through death" (Colossians 1:21–22). It is very wonderful to be reconciled.

Now, all of this is provided in our justification. If you feel distant from God, if you feel somehow or other there is a gulf between you and God, dear, brother or sister, God provided for you in your justification. There is no reason for it, no reason at all for it. You might be the blackest criminal in the world, but if you will only confess and you will only walk into the light, God will not only cleanse you, but you have your reconciliation. It is yours. God has provided for you.

When people hang their heads and say, "God won't speak to me," usually they need a bomb put behind them because normally there is something they will not put right, that's all. They will not walk in the light. Of course, it is their fault if there is a gulf, if they will not move. However, the provision is there. Take one step into the light and the blood of Jesus Christ will cleanse you instantly. If you get into the light you will be cleansed. There you are—reconciled. Not one single person has got to come into any gathering distanced from the Lord, with any barrier or with any gulf.

A Standing with God

Then there is standing. "For other foundation can no man lay than that which is laid, which is Jesus Christ" (1 Corinthians 3:11).

Our foundation is already there. You might build on it wood, hay, and stubble, but praise God, the foundation is there and you cannot do anything about that. If you are in Christ you are on the foundation, and the foundation is absolute acceptance with God, Jesus Christ.

"Having therefore, brethren, boldness to enter into the holy place by the blood of Jesus, by the way which he dedicated for us, a new and living way, through the veil, that is to say, his flesh; and having a great priest over the house of God; let us draw near with a true heart in fullness of faith, having our hearts sprinkled from an evil conscience" (Hebrews 10:19).

We have a standing with God. Every single one of us who is born of God's Spirit, has a standing with God. God has given us a standing and no one can take it away, no one, not even the devil. He cannot take it away from us. No one can take it away from us. We have a standing. This grace wherein we stand. Oh, how wonderful it all is!

Crucified—Christ As Us

The second aspect of the work of the cross of Calvary is that we are crucified, and I have entitled this "Christ as us." Christ not only died for us, but Christ died as us. He not only died in our place and bore our sin and bore the penalty of our sin and the wrath of God upon it, but when He died, He died as us. When He was buried, He was buried as us. When He was raised, He was raised as us. And when He was enthroned at God's right hand, He was enthroned as us. This is tremendous. This is the other side of the work of the cross.

> "I have been crucified with Christ; nevertheless I live, yet
> not I but Christ liveth in me: and the life which I now
> live, I live by the faith of the Son of God who loved
> me and gave Himself for me." Galatians 2:20

> "Knowing this, that our old man was crucified with him, that
> the body of sin might be done away, that so we should no longer
> be in bondage to sin; for he that hath died is justified from sin.
> But if we died with Christ, we believe that we shall also live
> with him; knowing that Christ being raised from the dead dieth
> no more; death no more hath dominion over him. For the death
> that he died, he died unto sin once; but the life that he liveth, he
> liveth unto God. Even so reckon ye also yourselves to be dead
> unto sin, but alive unto God in Christ Jesus." Romans 6:6–11

That is something tremendous!

> *"But far be it from me to glory, save in the cross of our*
> *Lord Jesus Christ, through which the world hath been*
> *crucified unto me, and I unto the world." Galatians 6:14*

This is a two-fold crucifixion. The world has been put on a cross and I have been put on another cross, so we cannot touch each other. That is the place to be, but not many of us are there. Nevertheless, that is what God has done in the cross.

> *"Ye died with Christ ... Having been buried*
> *with him." Colossians 2:20a, 12a*

So we died with Christ and we have been buried with Christ.

> *"If then ye were raised together with Christ, seek the things that*
> *are above, where Christ is seated on the right hand of God ...*
> *When Christ, who is our life, shall be manifested, then shall*
> *ye also with him be manifested in glory." Colossians 3:1, 4*

In this matter we come up against the problem of the self-life, and the self-nature, our old nature. We may be pardoned, we may be cleansed, we may be covered, we may be reconciled, we may have a standing with God, but we still have our old nature, and that is the problem. So what is going to happen? "Shall we continue in sin that grace may abound?" asks Paul. He has got it, and he understands only too fully the nature of the problem. If we had only justification, we would just go on happily sinning and grace will abound, but Paul says you cannot just do that. There is another side to the cross. How shall we continue in sin, we who died with Christ? And we have the whole problem of our self-life.

Our self-life is the problem. I do not know whether you have discovered that yet, but the biggest problem in the Christian life is the self-life; and the biggest problem in the church is the self-life. There is no doubt about it. We whine and we groan, but it is our self-life that is the problem all along. So having justified us and covered us, the painful work of removing what we are begins when once we see it. We do not have to have it removed now; we can wait, but sooner or later that operation takes place if we are going to go into the presence of God. For without holiness no man shall see the Lord. So we can wait for it, and I do not know exactly what will happen, but we will be saved so as by fire. Something tremendous will happen. We will get through, but saved by the skin of our teeth. However, God has made provision for us down here so that this whole life can be an education. This whole life can be, as it were, a sphere in which the self-life is dealt with and removed and Christ brought in. God does not want just to remove our self-life and leave us a kind of negative vacuum, an emptiness, and a void. He wants to bring Christ in in place of what we are, and this is the whole work of the cross.

The other aspect of the cross is the removal of the old in order to bring in the new, the removal of self for the bringing in of Christ. Now God has already done it at the cross, and you need not try to do it yourself. You cannot mortify your body. You cannot put your members to death. Do your best at this and you will find that you will get into a worse and worse state, until in the end you just give up altogether. You cannot do it. The whole point is God has done it.

Brother Nee used to use a beautiful illustration, which is the most helpful one I know of. If we take a little bit of paper and put it in a Bible, and we close the Bible and send that Bible to the other side of the world, the bit of paper in it goes with the Bible. Everything I do with that Bible is also done to the bit of paper. If I lift up the Bible, the paper is in the Bible. If I put the Bible down, the paper is in the Bible. If I put the Bible on the lectern, the piece of paper is in the Bible. If I put it on the chair, the piece of paper is on the chair.

God has put us in Christ, and when He crucified Christ, He crucified us, and when Christ was buried, we were buried. And when He raised Christ, we were raised, and when He enthroned Christ, we are enthroned. God has put us in Christ. It is so simple. But once the eyes of the heart open up to it and you see it, it is the beginning of something altogether new in your experience. You see we are dead, we are buried, and we are raised.

Buried with Christ

It is one thing to know you have been crucified; it is another thing to know that you have been buried. Some people know they have been crucified, but they are still there. I do not want to be vulgar, but you can see that they are there—putrefied, a corpse, and everyone around them is only too well aware that they are crucified. They have the smell of death around them. They have the whole atmosphere of death about them. It is all negative.

It is all sort of drab. It is all sad, dark, and colorless. And you cannot see Christ; you can only see them crucified, and whenever you touch them you feel like you are touching crucifixion. It is not the beauty of Christ; it is them. When Paul saw this he said, "Who shall deliver me from the body of this death?" He had the idea of gladiators bound together, one of whom would kill the other and could not be freed from him but would have to drag the dead body out with him. This is an awful thought and an awful picture. Do you know that is like a lot of us? We know what it is to be crucified with Christ; we have got that far. But oh dear, to change the illustration, the smell of burning is upon us when we come out of the fiery furnace. Everyone knows within a radius of a few miles that we have gone through a bad time and somehow or other the Lord has been taking us into the way of the cross.

Listen my dear friends, God has not only crucified us, He has buried us. This is not play-acting to hide the fact that we have been crucified. When you bury someone, you put them out of sight. You put them under the ground. They are out of sight. They are gone. They are finished. They are out of the way. You can only see the flowers and the daisies on the top. You cannot see them. They are gone. Buried. That is the wonder of it.

Raised with Christ

God has not only crucified us with Christ, buried us with Christ, but He has raised us with Christ. We have been raised to walk in newness of life. That means a freshness of life, always perennially fresh. Few of us know this. Many of us know something of the cross in this way, but there is a vast amount more yet for us to appropriate than what we have already appropriated. Even some of us who have seen it, and not all of us have seen it by any means, we have much more to see, to understand, and to claim, and appropriate. "Lord, I am not only crucified, I am buried. Now then cover it all and be the health of my countenance in this matter."

Brought to Zero at the Cross

What does God do with all that we are? This is the problem. What does God do? Some of you are going to serve the Lord. You have told the Lord you are ready to serve Him anywhere in the world. What is God going to do with you? Is He going to crucify the bad part of you and polish up the good part of you? Is it the part of you that is failing and sort of base that goes to the cross and the rest God is going to refine so it is a thing of beauty? What is God going to do with your talents and your gifts? What is He going to do with your zeal and your energy? I will tell you what this aspect of the cross means. It means that everything, all that you are comes to the altar and goes up in smoke. God terminates you at the altar. Your talents, your gifts, your good points, your bad points, all are crucified together with Christ and buried with Him. God brings everything to zero at the cross. Yes, everything! All that God is going to use has got to go through the cross and through the grave into resurrection and victory.

Let me explain very simply what I mean. You have a gift for playing the piano and this is a talent. You give it to the Lord.

You are going to serve Him, so you give it to Him. (I am just using this as an illustration.) You do not know anything about the cross and then one day you see it: "Oh, I am crucified with Christ." Then, slowly but surely your gift for playing the piano comes under the hammer of the cross. God starts to break all your self-confidence. He breaks all that you are and you lose everything you have. You are a talented person, but you have lost it all now. It has gone into the grave, finished. However, God does not leave it there. So often He will bring it through into resurrection and victory, and there is something about Christ in that talent that was never there before. Before the cross it was you; after the cross it is Christ.

You have a man like Paul with a genius of a brain, and what does God do with it? He breaks that man to pieces. He blinds him. He makes him look like a silly old fool being led by the hand into Damascus. He goes out to the desert. This man who sat at the feet of Gamaliel goes out to the desert like a hermit. In the end Paul comes back and he has lost a lot of his eloquence and he has lost a lot of the power of his mind, but now God uses his mind because it is Christ. And God can use that man's brain to give us the letters we have. We have to accept it. There is a brain there as well, but it is Christ in and through the brain. It is a crucified brain.

So you have zeal and energy; you have natural talents and gifts. Everything has to go to the cross, everything. All has to come to zero if it is to come through. This is what we mean by the work of the cross. It has all got to go through death and burial to resurrection and victory. It is the only way. We must see it, and then we must act.

Why did the Lord say in Matthew 16:24–25: "If any man will come after me, let him deny himself, take up his cross and follow me"? Did He mean that you have a little problem and that is your cross? Not at all; even though Luke actually says, "Let him take up his own cross." What the Lord means is this: each one of us has got to deliberately take up the cross. God will never put the cross on us. It is provided. God has put us on the cross, but He will leave it to every one of us to step in it. You and I have got to step deliberately. Luke puts it even more emphatically. He said, "Let each one take up his cross daily." And that is a deliberate act. Those crosses were heavy things, and the people going to the place of death had to carry them on their shoulders and drag them up the hill of Golgotha. It was a deliberate act. They did not just fall into it or drift into it; they had to really shoulder it. And you and I, once we have seen it, have to say, "Lord, I am committed. By faith I am committed to the cross, to the grave, to resurrection." That is the secret.

The whole point of this being crucified is that we might know what it is to be raised, and you cannot know resurrection until you are dead and buried. So until you have let go and gone down, then you will not know resurrection. So cry as you will, plead as you will, study as you will, work as you will, you will never know anything of the power of His resurrection until you are prepared for the cross and the grave. Never! There is an absolute veto on everything until you are prepared to go through the cross and the grave. Take that step and God will say to you immediately, "I will raise you. You let yourself go and I will raise you." Even the Lord Jesus had to learn that lesson on the cross.

The Fellowship of His Suffering

There is something else too, for there is a law of spiritual life and increase in this matter of being crucified. "Verily, verily, I say unto you, Except a grain of wheat fall into the earth and die, it abideth by itself alone; but if it die, it beareth much fruit" (John 12:24).

Now there is a law there and in II Corinthians 4:4–6 you will find the whole law and its outworking: death in us, life in you. That is a law for servants of God; it is an absolute law. Even if you know everything about the power of the Holy Spirit, you will still know a lot about carrying in your body the death of the Lord Jesus so there will be life in other people. Otherwise, all people will see is a lot of bounce. That's all. You have it all, but they do not. However, if they receive from you something, it is because you know death that they may know life. It is an absolute law all the time.

Again this is connected with the fellowship of His suffering: "That I may know Him, the power of His resurrection, the fellowship of His suffering, being made conformable unto His death" (Philippians 3:10). Paul speaks about filling up what is lacking of the afflictions of Christ (see Colossians 1:24). What an amazing thing! And it is all to do with being crucified.

I hope I have said enough about this side of the cross to touch a lot of problems, perhaps as many problems as there are people in this room. It is provided for you. You hate your self-life, do you? Have you got to the place where you loathe your self-life, but you cannot get rid of it? You haven't seen what the cross is. God has made provision for you, but you will not get anywhere first until you loathe yourself. Once you begin to loathe what you are you will say, "Why doesn't the Lord not deliver me?" In the end you will see. Only ask the Lord to enlighten the eyes of your heart.

Indwelt—Christ in Us

The third thing, which is the first aspect of the work of Pentecost, is indwelt. Christ in us is, of course, a part of our great salvation—Christ for us, Christ as us, Christ in us.

John 20:22: "And when he had said this, he breathed on them, and saith unto them, Receive ye the Holy Spirit." Receive ye the Holy Spirit.

Romans 8:9–11, 16, 26: "But ye are not in the flesh but in the Spirit, if so be that the Spirit of God dwelleth in you. But if any hath not the Spirit of Christ, he is none of his. And if Christ is in you, the body is dead because of sin; but the spirit is life because of righteousness. But if the Spirit of him that raised up Jesus from the dead dwelleth in you, he that raised up Christ Jesus from the dead shall give life also to your mortal bodies through his Spirit that dwelleth in you ... The Spirit himself beareth witness with our spirit, (that is within), that we are children of God ... And in like manner the Spirit also helpeth our infirmity: for we know not how to pray as we ought; but the Spirit himself maketh intercession for us with groanings which cannot be uttered." That is within.

"Christ in you, the hope of glory" (Colossians 1:27).

"That he would grant you, according to the riches of his glory, that ye may be strengthened with power through his Spirit

in the inward man; that Christ may dwell in your hearts
through faith; to the end that ye, being rooted and grounded
in love, may be strong to apprehend with all the saints what
is the breadth and length and height and depth, and to know
the love of Christ which passeth knowledge, that ye may be
filled unto all the fullness of God" (Ephesians 3:16–19).

There can be nothing truly practical and experimental without a knowledge of Christ's indwelling. You can have it all up in your mind until you realise that Christ is within. Until that moment arrives in your life it is head knowledge. Everything is bound up with a knowledge of Christ within practically. In other words you can be saved; legally, you are truly saved. Do not just despise that because it is legal. It is a true, actual, literal salvation. However, before that becomes practical and experimental and you begin to taste what salvation really is, know what it is to be being saved, until you actually know Christ within, you cannot know any of its practical outworking.

This is very, very important, for many Christians are woefully ignorant of Christ within. Everywhere, especially on the continents, in this matter you find people who know what it is to be justified, but they do not know anything of Christ within, Christ as our life and how vital it really is. We can know the work of the cross and become merely negative if we do not have a large appreciation and experience of Christ within. You cannot be clinical about these things. You can have someone who has really seen something of what it is to go to the cross, yet they have not fully appreciated the Christ within. Consequently, there is a sort of heaviness about it all because there is not that way for the Lord to bring them into the realisation of what it means to be raised in Christ. That is very important.

The only way that you and I can be brought into the realisation of all that God intends and promises is by the indwelling Spirit of God. Have you ever thought of all that Christ, all that God intends for us? Have you ever read in God's Word what a Christian should be? This is what God has promised. Look at this that He has shown us! Look at what God intends me to be—conformed to the image of His own Son. Then you wonder, how, how, how? The only way that it can be done is by the indwelling Spirit of God.

I must tell you a little story about a husband I knew who was very, very concerned about his wife because she was always getting very tired. He was an older man and very worried about his wife, so he had an idea to get a cleaner. He said, "You are far too tired and we must get someone in to help you with the cleaning." But do you know what happened? The wife would get up an hour early to go all over the house and clean because she didn't like the thought of the poor lady working too hard. So she would do the cleaning early. How silly! The lady was paid to do the work, but she was trying to do it for her.

This may seem a very silly illustration, but it is exactly what happens with many of us. God has put the Holy Spirit within us to live the Christian life, but many of us are desperately trying to do it. We are getting in the way of the Holy Spirit trying to do what He should be doing. Unless you and I see what it is to be crucified with Christ we get in the way. I cannot put it more simply.

"The fruit of the Spirit is love, joy, peace, longsuffering, kindness, goodness, faithfulness, meekness, self-control; against such there is no law. And they that are of Christ Jesus have crucified the flesh with the passions and the lusts thereof" (Galatians 5:22–24).

Fruit Bearing

It is one thing to crucify the flesh with the passions and lusts, but what about the fruit? The fruit of the Spirit is love, joy, peace. The whole point is that fruit comes from within. I know there is a lot else that happens to bring it into fruit, but it comes basically from within the tree, and you cannot make an oak tree bear apples. Suppose you tried. You could give it bags and bags of fertilizer. Oh, you could waste pounds and pounds pumping in fertilizer round the tree, thinking: "This ought to do it. This old tree will bear apples any time now that I am giving it plenty of rich food." It will not do anything of the kind. It can only bear acorns. You could get down and pray: "Oh, please make this tree have apples," but your prayer will not be answered, for the tree is an oak tree and God abides by laws in that matter. You might plead and try but it still will not bear apples. The whole point is that to bear apples it has to have apple life. The tree has got to be an apple tree with apple life, then it will bear apples.

In many ways this is where we make our great mistake. We try to think that the old man, the old nature, the old life in us can somehow or other bear the fruit of the Spirit, but it is the fruit of the Spirit which is love, joy, peace. It is not the fruit of me, but the fruit of the Spirit in my spirit, which is love, joy, peace.

So the thing I have to understand is that Christ is within me. If I see it, I can commit myself to it, and God can do the rest.

Reproduction of Christ

Realisation, reproduction of Christ is another thing to do with the indwelling.

> "But we all, with unveiled face beholding as in a mirror the glory of the Lord, are transformed into the same image from glory to glory, even as from the Lord the Spirit" (II Corinthians 3:18).

Do you see what is happening? In fact, we are being changed. How? By Christ within. That is how. I wish we could say it more clearly, but we are changed into the image of Christ by the Holy Spirit within. He is doing it. He is inside. You cannot do it. I cannot do it. All we can do is trust and obey, but God will do the work once we have seen it. We have to see it.

Union and Communion

And then there is union and communion. That is another thing bound up with the indwelling. Do you know what it is to be one with Christ, really one with Christ? Do you know what it is to walk hand in hand with Christ? You cannot walk hand in hand with Christ until you have seen that He is within. And when you have seen He is within, there is a comradeship, a fellowship, a union and a communion.

Oh, the tragedies that there are amongst us who are God's children in this matter! I know folk who say, "Would you pray for me?" And I say, "Why can't you pray?" "Oh well, I don't know whether the Lord hears me;" and when you get down to it, they say, "The Lord will not speak to me." Jesus said, "My sheep hear my voice," and there are some pretty poor sheep. But He says, "My sheep hear My voice." All the flock can hear His voice. They have a right to because they are His sheep. If only every one of us would really get to the Lord and see this question of indwelling, it would transform our lives. We would go to the Lord directly in prayer. We would listen for His voice ourselves, as well as having fellowship with others. Oh, it would make such a great difference! It is this whole matter of union and communion.

Empowered—Christ Upon Us

Lastly, there is this matter of being empowered—Christ upon us or Christ with us—it is rather difficult to get the right word. Christ upon us sounds a little archaic, but that is what it really means. It is Christ upon us as well as Christ behind us, but I do not want to give you the impression that it is "I" with the Lord's help. No, it is really Christ tabernacling upon us, enveloping us, absolutely, as it were, taking us in. He is upon us. This is what we call the empowering.

Acts 1:8: "But ye shall receive power, when the Holy Spirit is come upon you." Will you notice that in John 20:22 Jesus had already breathed upon them and said, "Receive ye the Holy Spirit." Why did He say that the Holy Spirit would come upon them when He had already breathed upon them and said, "Receive ye the

Holy Spirit"? I do not believe they did receive the Holy Spirit when Jesus breathed upon them. But what I do believe is that the Lord Jesus was trying to differentiate between two vital sides of the work of the Spirit—the indwelling when we receive the Spirit and the Holy Spirit coming upon us. These are the two distinct sides to the work of the Holy Spirit. When He came at Pentecost, of course it was the first time He came to dwell within them, but He also came upon them, and the two things work hand in hand. For our sakes, the Lord Jesus made this clear distinction when He said to them before the Holy Spirit was even given, "Receive ye the Holy Spirit." He wants them to be quite clear that there was this two-fold side to the work of the Holy Spirit.

In Ephesians 3:20 there is that little phrase: "according to the power that worketh in us." This is very wonderful. "Now unto him that is able to do exceeding abundantly above all that we ask or think." How few of us know anything of that—exceeding abundantly above all that we ask or think. To have a kind of experience of God like that—"according to the power that worketh in us." It is the appreciation of the power that is upon us and within us that is going to help us know something of "exceeding abundantly above what we ask or think."

"Now the God of hope fill you with all joy and peace in believing, that ye may abound in hope, in the power of the Holy Spirit" (Romans 15:13). There again there is joy and peace connected with the power of the Holy Spirit.

"I can do all things through Christ that strengtheneth me" (or makes me powerful) (Philippians 4:13).

"Go ye therefore, and make disciples of all the nations, and preach the gospel to all nations, baptizing them into the name of the Father and of the Son and of the Holy Spirit … and lo, I am with you always" (Matthew 28:19–20).

Why do you think the Lord Jesus said that? Was it a little text to be put up on walls to be seen everywhere, "Lo, I am with you always"? What do you think the Lord Jesus meant? No, He said, "Look here; this is your commission, this is your service. You are to be witnesses unto Me. I am with you. The risen Christ, the authority of Christ, the enthroned Christ—I am with you." This is the power of our service, and very few of us know anything about it. We are so quaking, we are so fearful, we are so retiring, we are so conscious, yet Jesus said, "Go and I am with you." Christ with us! He is not just behind us helping us, but He is empowering us to go to the whole world with the gospel. Very few of us, I am the same, know anything about this side of the work of the Holy Spirit—empowered.

The Baptism of the Spirit

This is often called the baptism of the Spirit, and because so many people talk about it, in the eyes of many, in erroneous ways, the whole thing is shelved and forgotten. Yet we bypass a vital truth if we just try to get round the question of the baptism of the Spirit. Yes, maybe you and I have the Holy Spirit. We have both His indwelling and His empowering the day we believed, but do we experience it? And if we do not experience it, what is the point of quibbling over words? We have to get into it, we have to find it, we have to discover it, and we have to appropriate it.

The whole point is that you can have the Holy Spirit within, and yet be so fearful, and so powerless, and so self-conscious.

You know you have Christ in you; you have seen it. The eyes of your heart have been enlightened and you know, yet you still tremble like a leaf. Look at those men in the upper room. They had bolted all the doors and they were quivering in fear. One hundred and twenty of them were behind locked doors "for fear of the Jews," it says. Even with the risen Christ, they did not unlock the doors. Have you noticed that? When the risen Christ was there in their midst they were only more fearful. They all shrank away and said they thought they had seen a spirit. He comforted them, but they did not unlock the doors until that day the Holy Spirit came upon them. I do not think anyone said, "Brother, unlock the door." Someone had already done it; possibly the Holy Spirit Himself, I do not know. But the doors were open and out they went, and the whole of Jerusalem heard. And that fearful man, Peter, who had denied His Lord with oaths and curses and had wept so bitterly afterwards, now stands up and preaches this great message. It is not much of a sermon frankly, if you look at it as sermons are supposed to be preached. It is a very poor sermon, but my word, three thousand people get saved. That is the kind of message it is. The man has got the Holy Spirit. This is what you and I need. It almost does not matter what the man says, however he uses Scripture; the Holy Spirit uses it. People get saved left, right, and center. That is just really what we need. This is what you and I need.

There is one other point about this. If anyone quibbles with me about this question of the empowering of the Holy Spirit, I want to point you to one other thing, which I believe is most significant. The Lord Jesus Christ, who was without sin, was born of the Spirit, and the Holy Spirit was within Him from the day He was born, yet when the Lord Jesus entered upon His ministry at thirty years of age, the Holy Spirit came upon Him. If the Lord Jesus had to know such an empowering of the Holy Spirit, how much more you and I need it. If one who is sinless and knew all about the indwelling of the Holy Spirit, if He had to know of the baptism of the Spirit, how much more should you and I know it. It is a very, very big point. People say to me: "Oh, I cannot pray; I pray at home. I could not possibly pray in the gathering." My dear brother, my dear sister, you need the Holy Spirit. It is as simple as that. You need the Holy Spirit to get on the inside of you, empower you; really empower you. You may know all about the indwelling of the Holy Spirit, but you have got to know all about the empowering of the Holy Spirit so that you are no longer self-conscious. You are carried out of yourself into Christ.

Of course, there are dangers, and traps, and snares. That is why we need to know what it is to be crucified with Christ; otherwise there are dangers. So we need to know deeply the indwelling of the Holy Spirit because there are such dangers in the empowering of the Holy Spirit. It is not for nothing that they were called men who were drunk. This seems to carry people almost out of their depths, out of self-consciousness to such an extent they do not know hardly what they are doing. I am not advocating that kind of thing, but I think it could do some of us a lot of good.

I am just saying that really and truthfully we have all this in Christ, but do we have it in experience? And it is no good just sitting forever in our seats saying, "I have it all, praise the Lord! Christ is mine. He has done it all." But in fact the Lord looks down from heaven and says, "Poor, poor, So-and-So, saying there they have it all. I have given them all, but they have not got it.

They have not stepped into it. What are they talking about? What are they singing about? They are not in the good of it." God wants to see us in the good of it.

Service

There are these three things to do with the empowering of the Holy Spirit. The first is service. "Ye shall be witnesses unto me when the Holy Spirit is come upon you." When you see power from on high, the Holy Spirit has come, and ye shall be witnesses unto Him. Isn't it interesting that the moment people receive this empowering of the Holy Spirit, they become witnesses. It is to do with witnessing and testimony and service.

In 1 Corinthians 12:4–11 you will find that every one of the gifts in the church is connected with the Holy Spirit. It is all by the Holy Spirit that you function, and if you don't know the empowering of the Holy Spirit, there is going to be a weakness of functioning. People are going to be holding back, and that is just what is happening in this company. There are gifts amongst us, gifts of ministry, many other kinds of gifts, and everyone is holding back. They are not empowered. And 1 Corinthians 12 tells us that the Holy Spirit is the key for this power to make us those who can serve the Lord.

In Exodus 35:30–31 we find a man called Bezalel. He was the man who was going to do all the cunning work, as the older version puts it so sweetly. And it says the Holy Spirit filled him and all his workers, and it was all to do with the house of God. It was service, and they were filled. In the Old Testament, again and again, when any man had a ministry or work to do, the Holy Spirit came upon him. Do distinguish between the Holy Spirit within and the Holy Spirit upon. There is a distinction and within that distinction lies something so vital to us all.

From Acts 2 onwards just see the triumph now of service that there is. They have their people like an Ananias and a Sapphira; they have Peter making dreadful mistakes publically and being rebuked, and a little public row with Paul. (I bet that caused a lot of gossip amongst them all, as they all talked of the day they heard Paul tell off Peter publically. Can you just hear them? Human nature is human nature.) They had their church at Corinth with its wickednesses and much else. They had their divisions at Philippi where the two ladies could not get on together, and many other things happening in various parts amongst God's people. They had all these problems, but the power of the Holy Spirit was so great that the church went right through in one generation till it had turned the Roman Empire upside down. And when in their thousands they went into the arena, the evil one could not destroy them. It had to be from within that the devil got the church down, through Constantine, from within. When the Holy Spirit was empowering them, Christ was with them, and they could go to their martyrdom joyfully because He was with them.

Possessing

I believe it is the key to overcoming, possession, and victory. In Joshua, when Joshua is at the beginning of possessing all that God has promised, he meets outside the walls of Jericho the Captain of the Lord's hosts, and He has a drawn sword. And we believe that is a symbol of the Holy Spirit. The Holy Spirit said,

"Now look here, Joshua, I want to get this abundantly clear; who is in charge, you or Me? And Joshua took off his shoes, bowed his head and said, "Lord." And they went forward and possessed. It is a picture for you and me. The Holy Spirit has got to go with us and before us in the possession of the land. Overcoming is linked with all this, and so is victory. We cannot possess God's fullness and purpose without the Spirit's empowering. I wish I could say more about that.

Sovereignty

Then there is sovereignty. In Acts 3:6 when Peter sees the crippled man, the Peter who just denied the Lord and run away from Him, he says to the man, with John: "Silver and gold have I none; but what I have, that give I thee. In the name of Jesus Christ of Nazareth, walk." There is authority. The man who had gone into the depths of despair was now experiencing the authority of God's Christ. How? By the empowering of the Holy Spirit. Pentecost had changed that man, absolutely changed him.

In Acts 4:30–31 it says the church prayed and they said, "Lord, do You know what they are doing? They told Peter he is not to speak anymore in Your name. Lord, stretch forth thine arm and let signs and wonders be done in the name of Thy Holy Child Jesus." And the place was shaken where they were, and they were filled with the Holy Spirit. God said, "All right, I am with you. I am with you." They had another little Pentecost, that's all, just another little taste of Pentecost. And on they went with Christ. I could say so much more, but I am going to leave it. It is the fourth thing in our salvation and for the want of it in our experience,

I believe many of us are very conscious of much that is lacking, a powerlessness, and a fearfulness. We need it.

What can we say to all of that? We have got to experience more of Christ. There is always more of Christ for us. God has given us Christ—not part of Christ, not most of Christ, but all of Christ. And we can know Him in this four-fold way—Christ for us, Christ as us, Christ in us, Christ with us. He is there to be known, there to be experienced, all the provision. If you want to know the fullness of God, then you have got to experience all four, and you have got to experience all four of these matters in an ever-increasing way. Come back to them again and again. Don't think you can have a blessed experience twenty-five years ago that will take you right the way through your life. It will not do anything of the kind. You will have to go back again and again and again and learn more deeply and appropriate more fully what God has done.

For those of you who are going to serve the Lord in any way, in the end it is not what you preach and it is not what you teach that matters so much. It is what you are experiencing. And what the world wants to see and what young believers want to see are not people who can preach so much, as people in whom they see something of what those people believe being worked out. They are experiencing it. With all their failure and with all that they are naturally, they are experiencing what they preach. It is a very, very high calling and might well make us fear, but God has made all the provision and given it to us. Let's go in and possess what is ours in Christ. Let's get back to the Lord and say, "Lord, that is what I need." There is certainly, maybe one thing here that stands out in your heart and mind, maybe more. I don't know. Go home and get on your knees and say, "Lord, open the eyes of my heart to see this matter. Help me to appropriate by faith what is mine."

Shall we pray:

Lord Jesus, we do pray that Thou would not allow this to be just a study, but we pray together that by Thy Spirit Thou will help every one of us really to go back and be honest with Thee. Lord, open the eyes of our hearts that we might really see these things. We ask Thee to make us a people who really appropriate what Thou hast given and provided in Christ. And we ask it together in Thy name. Amen.

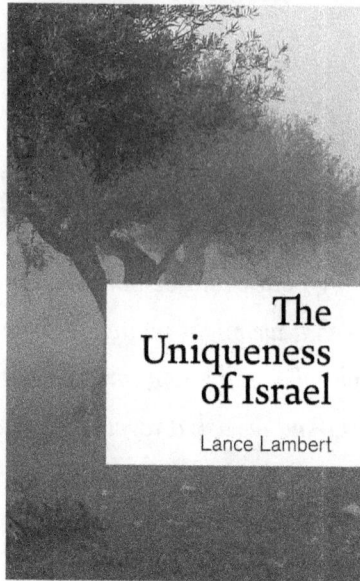

The
Uniqueness
of Israel

Lance Lambert

The Uniqueness of Israel

Woven into the fabric of Jewish existence there is an undeniable uniqueness. There is bitter controversy over the subject of Israel, but time itself will establish the truth about this nation's place in God's plan. For Lance Lambert, the Lord Jesus is the key that unlocks Jewish history He is the key not only to their fall, but also to their restoration. For in spite of the fact that they rejected Him, He has not rejected them.

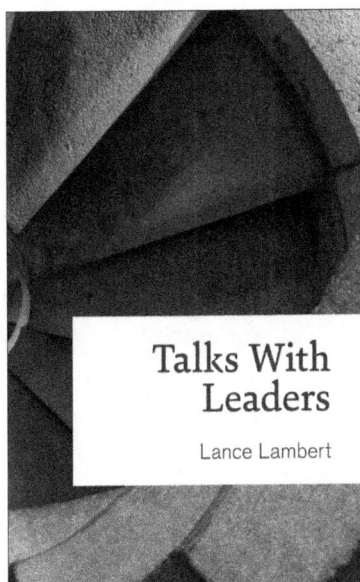

Talks With
Leaders

Lance Lambert

Talks With Leaders

"O Timothy, guard that which is committed unto thee ..."
(1 Timothy 6:20) Has God given you something? Has God
deposited something in you? Is there something of Himself
which He has given to you to contribute to the people of God?
Guard it. Guard that vision which He has given you. Guard that
understanding that He has so mercifully granted to you. Guard
that experience which He has given that it does not evaporate or
drain away or become a cause of pride. Guard that which the Lord
has given to you by the Holy Spirit. In these heart-to-heart talks
with leaders Lance Lambert covers such topics as the character
of God's servants, the way to serve, the importance of anointing,
and hearing God's voice. Let us consider together how to remain
faithful with what has been entrusted to us.

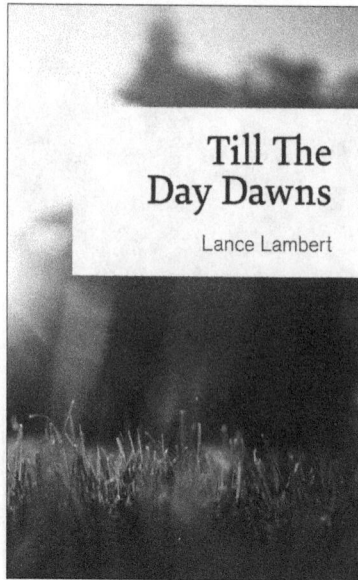

Till the Day Dawns

"And we have the word of prophecy made more sure; whereunto ye do well that ye take heed, as unto a lamp shining in a dark place, until the day dawn, and the day-star arise in your hearts." (II Peter 1:9).

The word of prophecy was not given that we might merely be comforted but that we would be prepared and made ready. Let us look into the Word of God together, searching out the prophecies, that the Day-Star arise in our hearts until the Day dawns.

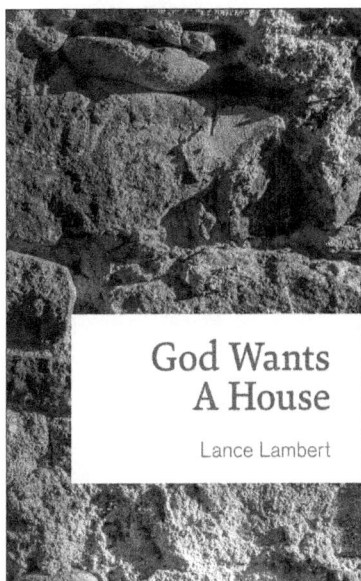

God Wants
A House

Lance Lambert

God Wants a House

Where is God at home? Is He at home in Richmond, VA? Is He at home in Washington? Is He at home in Richmond, Surrey? Is He at home in these other places? Where is God at home? There are thousands of living stones, many, many dear believers with real experience of the Lord, but where has the ark come home? Where are the staves being lengthened that God has finally come home? In God Wants a House Lance looks into this desire of the Lord, this desire He has to dwell with His people. What would this dwelling look like? Let's seek the Lord, that we can say with David, "One thing have I asked of Jehovah, that will I seek after: that I may dwell in the house of Jehovah all the days of my life, To behold the beauty of Jehovah, And to inquire in his temple."